A Book You'll Actually Read

On Church Leadership

Mark Driscoll

CROSSWAY BOOKS

WHEATON, ILLINOIS

On Church Leadership
Copyright © 2008 by Mark Driscoll

Published by Crossway Books
    a publishing ministry of Good News Publishers
    1300 Crescent Street
    Wheaton, Illinois 60187

Interior design and typesetting by Lakeside Design Plus
Cover design and illustration by Patrick Mahoney
First printing 2008

Printed in the United States of America

Scripture quotations are from *The Holy Bible, English Standard Version*®, copyright © 2001 by Crossway Bibles, a publishing ministry of Good News Publishers. Used by permission. All rights reserved.

Trade Paperback ISBN: 978-1-4335-0137-1
PDF ISBN: 978-1-4335-0440-2
Mobipocket ISBN: 978-1-4335-0441-9

Library of Congress Cataloging-in-Publication Data
Driscoll, Mark, 1970–
    On church leadership / Mark Driscoll.
        p. cm. — (A book you'll actually read)
      Includes bibliographical references (p.).
      ISBN 978-1-4335-0137-1 (tpb)
      1. Christian leadership. I. Title. II. Series.

    BV652.1.D74 2008
    262'.1—dc22

                                  2008000489

VP	16	15	14	13	12	11	10	09	08
	9	8	7	6	5	4	3	2	1

Contents

Series Introduction

On Church Leadership is part of an ongoing series of books you will actually read. The average person can read these books (minus the appendixes) in roughly one hour. The hope is that the big truths packed into these little books will make them different from the many other books that you would never pick up or would pick up only to quickly put down forever because they are simply too wordy and don't get to the point.

The A Book You'll Actually Read series is part of the literature ministry of Resurgence, called Re:Lit. Resurgence (www.theresurgence.com) is a growing repository of free theological resources, such as audio and video downloads, and includes information about conferences we host. The elders of Mars Hill Church (www.marshillchurch. org) have generously agreed to fund Resurgence along with the Acts 29 Church Planting Network (www.acts29network.org) so that our culture can be filled with a resurgence of timeless Christian truth that is expressed and embodied in timely cultural ways. Free downloads of audio and/or video sermons by Pastor Mark Driscoll on topical issues and entire books of the Bible are available at www.marshillchurch.org.

Introduction

In the fall of 1996 we officially launched Mars Hill Church in Seattle. I was twenty-five years of age and had been a Christian since the age of nineteen. Our city was among the least churched in the nation, with more dogs than either children or Christians. Our church was about as big as a Mormon family. Our budget was meager. Our leadership structure was informal. And, as a result, our ministry was painful.

In the first few years our church experienced a great number of tensions. Many of them were about conflicting theological beliefs on everything from the Bible to Jesus, hell, women in ministry, mode of baptism, and the return of Jesus, which I hoped would happen soon so I could get out of the mess I had made by starting a church.

Without formal leaders and structures in place, it was not long before the most vocal, networked, and pushy people started asserting themselves as leaders of our little church and causing a great amount of division. Their varying demands quickly sidetracked the mission of our church to love our city and see it transformed by the power of Jesus. Our internal church strife quickly overshadowed our external cultural mission.

At the root of all of our troubles was the issue of authority. Our people, most of whom were young in both age and faith, did not have a biblical understanding of or respect for authority. The issue of authority begins with Jesus himself. During his earthly ministry, those who heard Jesus teach were astonished by his authority,[1] which included the authority to forgive sins,[2] cast out demons,[3] heal sickness,[4] and mete out

1. Matt. 7:28–29.
2. Matt. 9:6–8.
3. Mark 3:15.
4. Luke 9:1.

our eternal judgment.[5] After his resurrection from death, Jesus said, "All authority in heaven and on earth has been given to me."[6]

Today, Jesus is seated on his throne in heaven as glorious, exalted, and supreme King, Lord, and God in authority. There is not one inch of creation, one culture or subculture of people, one lifestyle or orientation, one religion or philosophical system that he does not possess full authority over. Jesus is in the place of highest authority, as Paul says, "For in him the whole fullness of deity dwells bodily, and you have been filled in him, who is the head of all rule and authority."[7] The authority of governments and rulers,[8] husbands,[9] parents,[10] bosses,[11] and church leaders[12] all proceed from Jesus.

Not only does Jesus possess all authority, but while on the earth he also gave us the perfect model of what it means to respect authority. On this point, 1 Corinthians 11:3 says, "But I want you to understand that the head of every man [or husband] is Christ, the head of a wife is her husband, and the head of Christ is God." The meaning of the word "head" in this verse has been hotly debated. But its most common use in Scripture is in reference to a position of authority. Jesus is called the head of the church because he has authority over the church.[13] If Jesus is not our highest authority, then who is?

Furthermore, Jesus is ruling today through the authority of both Scripture and God the Holy Spirit, who has been sent to teach us Scripture and empower us for

5. John 5:27.
6. Matt. 28:18.
7. Col. 2:9–10.
8. Rom. 13:1; 1 Pet. 2:13.
9. 1 Pet. 3:1–7.
10. Ex. 20:12.
11. Col. 3:22–25.
12. Heb. 13:17.
13. Eph. 1:10, 22; 4:15; 5:23; Col. 1:18; 2:10, 19.

obedient, regenerated lives. Scripture itself claims to be God-breathed or inspired: "All Scripture is breathed out by God and profitable for teaching, for reproof, for correction, and for training in righteousness, that the man of God may be competent, equipped for every good work."[14] Jesus himself also taught that "Scripture cannot be broken."[15] This is because the Scriptures are from God and therefore come with his authority and power. Furthermore, the early church treated the apostles' New Testament teaching as authoritative, just as it did the Old Testament teaching of the prophets.[16] Because of this we are told that the church is "built on the foundation of the apostles [New Testament] and prophets [Old Testament], Christ Jesus himself being the cornerstone."[17] Subsequently, Christians, including myself, rightly believe that Scripture (Old and New Testaments) is our highest authority, or metaphorical Supreme Court, by which all other things are tested. Practically, this means that lesser courts of reason, tradition, and culture are under the highest court of truth, which is divinely inspired Scripture. During the Protestant Reformation, the slogans *sola Scriptura* and *prima Scriptura* they became popular to summarize this conviction; they mean Scripture alone is our highest authority. This should not be confused with *solo Scriptura*, which is the erroneous belief that truth is only to be found in Scripture and nowhere else. Scripture itself tells us that God reveals truth to us in such things as creation and our conscience, but that the beliefs we may subscribe to from such forms of lesser revelation are to be tested by Scripture.

Therefore, Jesus is our example of how we should both act when we are in authority and react when we are under authority. First Corinthians 11:3 is one of the key texts for what theologians call *functional subordinationism*. It is the biblical teaching that

14. 2 Tim. 3:16–17.
15. John 10:35.
16. Acts 2:42; 15.
17. Eph. 2:20.

our Trinitarian God exists as a community of equals with different roles and deference for authority within the Trinity. For example, throughout his life we see Jesus
constantly speaking of his submission to the authority of God the Father; Jesus continually states that the Father sent him to earth on his mission and that he was doing
what the Father told him to do and saying what the Father told him to say. Other
Scriptures also illustrate this principle, showing how Jesus Christ recognized the authority of God the Father while remaining equal to God the Father.[18]

While the authority of Jesus is always perfect, earthly authorities can at times be
imperfect. If an authority is indeed acting sinfully and breaking the laws of a higher
authority, rather than abandoning authority systems altogether, we should appeal to
a higher authority for justice. For example, a husband is to both submit to the authority of God and his church leaders as Jesus submitted to authority, and also exercise
authority over his family in a way that is loving and gracious like Jesus exercises his
authority. However, if that man should become harsh with his wife or children, they
should appeal to the higher authorities of church leadership and God's Word for justice. The answer to abusive authority is not an absence of authority but rather righteous
authority that rules under the authority of Scripture and Jesus. The right response to
abusive authority can be calling the church and even the police. Sadly, it is all too
common that people in the church are guilty of the sin of Diotrephes, "who likes to
put himself first, [and] does not acknowledge our authority."[19]

Anyway, getting back to our struggling little church of anarchy and dissent, it was
at that time when I realized that I needed to install qualified leaders and empower
them with the authority to help lead the church by disciplining some people, kicking
others out, training the teachable, encouraging the broken, empowering other leaders,

18. John 3:17; 4:34; 6:38; 8:29; 12:49.
19. 3 John 9.

and reaching the lost before the lunatics completely overtook the asylum/church plant. We needed leaders so we could execute our mission of bringing the gospel of Jesus to our city in word and deed.

The obvious need for biblically based, formal, and qualified leadership led me on a lengthy study of how a church should be organized. I had never been a pastor in a church or even a formal member of any church in my life. So, I studied Scripture, read dozens of books on church government (which was as exciting as watching ice melt), read dozens more books on church history and Christian movements, and met with pastors of various churches to hear how they were organized.

In the end, I arrived at what I believed was a model of church government that was both biblically sound and practically effective. I taught our little church on these matters, and before long we had implemented the kind of church government that I was convicted was most faithful. Immediately, our church began to grow in both health and size.

However, many of the people who attended Sunday services with us in the early days left the church because they were unwilling to submit to any spiritual authority. Many do not attend church anywhere, and some have even stopped claiming to be Christians. Others have matured in their faith and returned to our church, where they respect respectable authority and have been a blessing because of their humility and teachable disposition.

To help our people understand how we are governed, I wrote a booklet that we published internally to answer their questions. Over the years, many thousands of these booklets have been given away by our church for our people to read and share with friends and leaders of other churches. After visiting our church, my friends at Crossway asked if I would be willing to rewrite and expand the booklet, which was a humbling honor. I have rewritten that booklet, and the result is this small book. My hope was to boil down some of the big concepts regarding church leadership into a manageable and understandable format. The average person should be able to read this entire book in roughly one hour. You will not read a bunch of cute stories about bunny rabbits giving their lives to Jesus and such because I do not want to waste any of my words or any of your time. My hope is that through this book, Jesus would be honored, churches would be well served, and lost people would meet Jesus and grow in their love for him and his bride, the church.

1

Pastor Jesus

Before we can discuss church leadership, we must first define what we mean by "church." The church is the community of all Christians throughout history who have been loved and saved by Jesus Christ,[1] including the believing people of the Old Testament.[2] In every church, there are people who are not Christians,[3] including both lost people and wolves sent by Satan to lead people astray.[4] While it is possible for Christians to know who else is a Christian (e.g., those people who use frequent references to Christian brothers and sisters), ultimately only the Lord knows exactly who is and is not a Christian.[5] In this sense, "church" refers to every person of any age, race, and culture whose sins are forgiven through the death and resurrection of Jesus Christ; this is commonly called the "universal church."

The various congregations of the universal church that meet together for such things as teaching, fellowship, and worship are commonly called the "local church."[6] In fact, many of the letters in the New Testament were written to help inform and direct the local churches of such cities as Philippi, Corinth, Ephesus, Colossae, and Thessalonica. Both the Old and New Testaments were written to communities of

1. Acts 20:28; Eph. 5:25.
2. Deut. 4:10; Acts 7:38; Heb. 2:12, cf. Ps. 22:22.
3. Matt. 13:24–30.
4. Acts 20:29–30.
5. 2 Tim. 2:19.
6. For example, see Heb. 10:25.

God's people who regularly gathered together for such meetings, to help inform and direct their lives together as the family of God on mission to see Jesus transform their cities. The Bible is clear that every Christian is a part of the larger church body and is expected to participate in the life of a local church with the gift(s) God has given him or her. This is so that God may be glorified and so his people may be built up through their service to one another.[7] It is therefore a sin for someone who claims to be a Christian to not be actively loving his or her Christian brothers and sisters[8] and seeking to build up the church as faithful members of a church.[9]

The Scriptures are clear that Jesus Christ is the head of the church.[10] Jesus is the Apostle who plants a church.[11] Jesus is the Leader who builds the church.[12] Jesus is the Senior Pastor and Chief Shepherd who rules the church.[13] And it is ultimately Jesus who closes churches down when they have become faithless or fruitless.[14] Therefore, it is absolutely vital that a church loves Jesus, obeys Jesus, imitates Jesus, and follows Jesus at all times and in all ways, according to the teaching of his Word.[15]

Human leadership in the church is little more than qualified Christians who are following Jesus and encouraging other people to follow them as they follow Jesus. Because of this, church leaders must be good sheep who follow their Chief Shepherd Jesus well before they are fit to be shepherds leading any of his sheep. This is in large part what Paul meant when he told Christians in various local churches to "be imita-

7. 1 Cor. 12:1–31.
8. 1 John 1:7; 3:17–18; 4:21.
9. 1 Cor. 12:7; 14:6, 12, 26b.
10. Eph. 1:9, 22–23; 4:15; 5:23.
11. Heb. 3:1.
12. Matt. 16:18.
13. 1 Pet. 5:4.
14. Rev. 2:5.
15. Col. 3:16.

tors of me, as I am of Christ."[16] While it may seem obvious to insist that any discussion of church leadership begin with the centrality and preeminence of Jesus, sadly, many churches omit him from their organizational charts altogether. At the risk of stating the obvious, every church must place Jesus Christ in the position of highest authority and devotion in both the organizational chart and the life of the church.

Serving under Jesus are elders, deacons, and church members. Philippians 1:1 illustrates this church leadership structure: "Paul and Timothy, servants of Christ Jesus, To all the saints in Christ Jesus who are at Philippi, with the overseers and deacons." Packed in this verse we discover the three kinds of leaders who take responsibility for the health and progress of the local church. We will spend some time investigating each of their roles. First, there are elders ("overseers" in this verse), who are the senior leadership in the church. Second, there are deacons, who function as pastoral assistants by also leading the church alongside the elders. Third, there are "saints," or Christians, who love God and help lead the local church by using their resources (time, talent, and treasure) to help build up their church as church members. In the remainder of this book we will examine each of these groupings as well as the role of women in local church leadership.

16. 1 Cor. 11:1.

2

Elders

Elders are the male leaders of the church who are synonymously called pastors, bishops, and overseers throughout the New Testament.[1] While the various words are used interchangeably, they each refer to a different aspect of the same role in the same office. As an elder, a man has rank and authority to rule and govern a church. As a bishop, he has the responsibility before God to rule and protect a church. As a pastor, he has the high honor of caring for Christians and evangelizing non-Christians. As an overseer, he has the responsibility before God of leading and managing the church. Therefore, when the Bible uses words like elder, bishop, pastor, overseer, and such, don't get too nit-picky and try to figure out which word applies to the old man in a dress with a big hat on his head and a phat ring on his finger, but accept that sometimes one guy has a few titles, like I do as a poppa/daddy/father.

The elders are men chosen for their ministry according to clear biblical requirements after a sufficient season of testing in the church.[2] Elders are nearly always spoken of in plurality because God intends for more than one man to lead and rule over the church, as a safeguard for both the church and the man.

The Bible defines the qualifications of an elder in two primary places (1 Tim. 3:1–7; Titus 1:5–9), and the lists are virtually identical. Three things are noteworthy about this list. First, the list is really about men being good Christians, assuming that good Christians will make good pastors. This is curious because too many

1. Acts 20:28; Eph. 4:11; 1 Pet. 5:2.
2. 1 Tim. 2:11–3:7; Titus 1:5–9.

pastors are not very good Christians. Second, the qualifications for a pastor are in large part tied not to his work at the church, but rather to whether or not he has been a good pastor in his home with his family and in his world with his neighbors and coworkers; too many pastors are good pastors at the expense of being good husbands, fathers, neighbors, and the like. Third, establishing whether or not a man actually meets these criteria requires relational time in community over a long season because the list is about counting character, which is more difficult than counting rocks, as one pastor has quipped. To help you understand these qualifications, I will briefly list and explain them from their appearance in 1 Timothy.

1 Timothy 3:1–7

The saying is trustworthy: If anyone aspires to the office of overseer, he desires a noble task. Therefore an overseer must be above reproach, the husband of one wife, sober-minded, self-controlled, respectable, hospitable, able to teach, not a drunkard, not violent but gentle, not quarrelsome, not a lover of money. He must manage his own household well, with all dignity keeping his children submissive, for if someone does not know how to manage his own household, how will he care for God's church? He must not be a recent convert, or he may become puffed up with conceit and fall into the condemnation of the devil. Moreover, he must be well thought of by outsiders, so that he may not fall into disgrace, into a snare of the devil.

Seventeen Qualifications of an Elder-Pastor from 1 Timothy 3:1–7

Relation to God

1. A man: a masculine leader, a dudely dude
2. Above reproach: without any character defect
3. Able to teach: effective Bible communicator
4. Not a new convert: mature Christian

Relation to Family

   5. Husband of one wife: one-woman man, sexually pure (this does not require a man to be married, as Paul, Timothy, Jesus, and widowed men could qualify)

   6. Submissive children: successful father

   7. Manages family well: provides for, leads, organizes, loves

Relation to Self

   8. Sober-minded: mentally and emotionally stable

   9. Self-controlled: disciplined life of sound decision-making

  10. Not a drunkard: without addictions

  11. Not a lover of money: financially content and upright

Relation to Others

  12. Respectable: worth following and imitating

  13. Hospitable: welcomes strangers, especially non-Christians, for evangelism

  14. Not violent: even-tempered

  15. Gentle: kind, gracious, loving

  16. Not quarrelsome: peaceable, not divisive or contentious

  17. Well thought of by outsiders: respected by non-Christians

In summary, only men of the finest character are fit for leadership in God's church. One pastor has quipped that many young men raised on the apron strings of their Mother the Church aspire to vocational ministry because it is an indoor job that does not require any heavy lifting. But Paul tells a young pastor named Timothy that to be a pastor means you can pull the load of an ox,[3] fight like a warrior,[4] live a life of

3. 1 Tim. 5:17–18.
4. 2 Tim. 2:3–4.

discipline to compete with the skill of an athlete,[5] and work tirelessly like a farmer who is up before the sun doing his job every day.[6]

According to the Bible, formal theological training is not required, though such training can indeed be very beneficial. A salary is also not required, though an elder-pastor is worth an honorable wage.[7]

Elders are not ultimately nominated by committees or congregational votes, but rather called by God himself. Paul tells elders that "the Holy Spirit has made you overseers."[8] Once called by God, a man must then examine his own life and family to see if he meets the qualifications of an elder. If he does not, then a lengthy season of repentant living and transformation are required before there is any talk of him becoming a pastor. If/when a man is qualified, he then needs to have a personal desire to accept the work and responsibility of eldership and nominate himself to the other elders as a candidate for eldership consideration. On this point, 1 Timothy 3:1 says, "If anyone aspires to the office of overseer, he desires a noble task."

Upon nominating himself as an elder candidate, a formal process of testing his calling must be undertaken. This process should include examining his family, financial giving to the church, performance at work, relationship with people outside the church, service in the church, spiritual gifts, ministry passions, attitude toward authority, work ethic, leadership gifts, humility, and anything and everything else related to his conversion, calling, character, courage, and competency. If the man is unanimously confirmed as a called and qualified elder by the other elders, he should then be brought before the church in some notifying way so that the people in the church have an opportunity to raise any concerns or questions they have about the

5. 2 Tim. 2:5.
6. 2 Tim. 2:6.
7. 1 Tim. 5:17–18.
8. Acts 20:28.

man's eldership nomination. If there is no disqualifying opposition to the man, then he should be voted in by the other elders and installed as an elder by the laying of hands by the other elders as Scripture states.[9]

The issue of which men lead the church is of the utmost seriousness, because both the reputation of the gospel in the community and the health of the church are contingent upon godly, qualified men who keep in step with Jesus and who can lead the church to do likewise. The elders function as an accountable team, much like Jesus' first disciples, and they are therefore quite unlike secular notions of a business or nonprofit organizational board.

In addition to the qualifications of an elder, the Bible also provides the duties of elders-pastors:

- Praying and studying Scripture[10]
- Ruling/leading the church[11]
- Managing the church[12]
- Caring for people in the church[13]
- Giving account to God for the church[14]
- Living exemplary lives[15]
- Rightly using the authority God has given them[16]

9. 1 Tim. 4:14; 5:22.
10. Acts 6:4.
11. 1 Tim. 5:17.
12. 1 Tim. 3:4–5.
13. 1 Pet. 5:2–5.
14. Heb. 13:17.
15. Heb. 13:7.
16. Acts 20:28.

- Teaching the Bible correctly[17]
- Preaching[18]
- Praying for the sick[19]
- Teaching sound doctrine and refuting false teachings[20]
- Working hard[21]
- Rightly using money and power[22]
- Protecting the church from false teachers[23]
- Disciplining unrepentant Christians[24]
- Obeying the secular laws as the legal ruling body of a corporation[25]
- Developing other leaders and teachers[26]

This final point is often overlooked. An elder is not someone who is a helper that does a lot of work for the church, because that is the definition of a deacon. Rather, an elder is a leader who trains other leaders to lead various aspects of the church. Therefore, no man should be an elder unless he can effectively train people to not only be mature Christians, but mature Christians leaders who train other leaders.

17. Eph. 4:11; 1 Tim. 3:2.
18. 1 Tim. 5:17.
19. James 5:13–15.
20. Titus 1:9.
21. 1 Thess. 5:12.
22. 1 Pet. 5:1–3.
23. Acts 20:17–31.
24. Matt. 18:15–17.
25. Rom. 13:1–7.
26. Eph. 4:11–16; 2 Tim. 2:1–2.

First among Equals

Leading the elders under the rule of Jesus must be a senior elder who is first among equals and is responsible to help train the elders who train additional leaders. People often resist believing any hierarchy within the elder team is biblical; they see any hierarchy within the elders as demeaning of some elders because they are unequal to the other elders. Yet Alexander Strauch, who has written the most thorough book on biblical eldership, points out that

> Failure to understand the concept of "first among equals" (or 1 Timothy 5:17) has caused some elderships to be tragically ineffective in their pastoral care and leadership. Although elders act jointly as a council and share equal authority and responsibility for the leadership of the church, all are not equal in their giftedness, biblical knowledge, leadership ability, experience, or dedication. Therefore, those among the elders who are particularly gifted leaders and/or teachers will naturally stand out among the other elders as leaders and teachers within the leadership body.[27]

The following lines of reasoning show that the pattern of both equality and hierarchy is common throughout Scripture:[28]

- Within the Godhead we see Jesus doing the Father's will and speaking the Father's words in clear deference to the Father, though they are equal and united as one.

27. Alexander Strauch, *Biblical Eldership* (Littleton, CO: Lewis and Roth, 1995), 45.
28. The following points are summarized from chapter 26 of Gene Getz's *Elders and Leaders* (Chicago: Moody Press, 2003).

- In the government of the home (after which the government of the church is patterned), we see that husbands and wives are equal as God's image-bearers and that the husband is in leadership as the head of the family.
- Within the church we see that Jesus chose Peter, James, and John as his inner circle of disciples who were present at particular times when the other disciples were not (e.g., on the Mount of Transfiguration). They were given access to Jesus, such as sitting next to him at meals, in the place of honor and leadership among the apostles.
- Before he ascended, Jesus clearly appointed Peter as the leader of the disciples, and he became the dominant figure throughout the Gospels and the book of Acts until his death. John functioned as the second leader in command and ascended to first position following Peter's death. Chart 2.1 indicates this, as does the simple observation that we know virtually nothing about some apostles who were obviously godly and important but not prominent.
- Peter, James, and John are mentioned first among the lists of the New Testament apostles since they are the leaders among the men.
- Peter also functioned as the leader of James and John in their business together before Jesus appointed them to be apostles.[29]
- In the upper room after Jesus' ascension, Peter stood up among the believers and spoke because he was their leader as appointed by Jesus.[30]
- On the day of Pentecost it was Peter who stepped forward from among the apostles to preach the gospel as their leader.[31]

29. Luke 5:7, 10.
30. Acts 1:15.
31. Acts 2:14.

Chart 2.1 *Disciple Appearances in the New Testament*

Apostle	Number of appearances in the Gospels	Number of appearances in the book of Acts	Total appearances
Peter	117	72	189
John	35	15	50
James	16	2	18
Philip	16	1	17
Andrew	12	1	13
Thomas	10	1	11
Matthew/Levi	8	1	9
James, son of Alphaeus	6	1	7
Thaddeus/ Judas	3	1	4
Simon the Zealot	3	1	4
Bartholomew/ Nathaniel	0	1	1
Judas Iscariot	20	2	22

- Peter referred to himself as a "fellow elder" though he was the leader of the elders.[32]
- Initially, Barnabas led a missions team in Acts with Paul and John Mark as his assistants, but in a short time they came to be known as "Paul and his companions,"[33] because Paul had overtaken Barnabas in leadership promi-

32. 1 Pet. 5:1.
33. Acts 13:13.

nence, a fact further proven by Paul's penning of New Testament books, not Barnabas's.

- In Jerusalem, Jesus' brother James was clearly seen as the primary leader,[34] which is also shown by his penning of the epistle bearing his name; none of the other elders in Jerusalem wrote New Testament books.
- Both Timothy and Titus are widely recognized as senior leaders, even being told by Paul to "appoint elders,"[35] which indicates their authority over those elders they appoint.

In summary, men like Peter, John, Paul, Timothy, and Titus are obviously prominent leaders in the New Testament who exercise authority over other elders without being overbearing or sinful in the exercise of their necessary authority.

Therefore, for an elder team to function effectively, it must have a called, qualified, gifted, devoted, humble, and competent senior human leader who leads the elder team and helps guard the gate for new elders joining the team to ensure unity and success. To do his job, that man must not have blind obedience or complete unaccountable authority. Rather, he must have the freedom, trust, authority, respect, honor, and support of the elders and other church leaders to actually lead the church. If not, there can be no leadership; leaders will no longer lead the entire church working on behalf of the best interests of the gospel, but will become representatives of various agendas, departments, factions, and programs in the church. Without a senior leader, dissention will come as people fight over resources; there will not be decisions, but compromises, which are the death of the church.

34. Acts 12:17; 15:7–11, 13–21; 21:18.
35. Titus 1:5.

As a general rule, the best person to hold the position of first among equals is the primary preaching pastor. Indeed, 1 Timothy 5:17 says, "Let the elders who rule well be considered worthy of double honor, especially those who labor in preaching and teaching." While all elders deserve respect and honor, this is especially true of the primary preaching pastor and, as the context of this verse shows, part of that honoring often includes the highest salary of all paid elders. The pulpit is the most visible place of exercised authority in the church. As such, only qualified elders should preach, which can include welcoming qualified elders from other churches from time to time as appropriate.

Principles and Methods

One of the key roles of the senior leader is to help ensure that the elders are organized in an effective manner. The New Testament is very clear on the functions of elders (e.g., leading, disciplining, teaching, shepherding, praying) and the qualifications of an elder.[36] However, the New Testament is not clear on the form of the elders. This is because the form must be adapted for the various cultures that have now had elders for two thousand years. The New Testament does not tell us how many elders a local church should have, how often they should meet, how they should conduct their vote (e.g., unanimity, consensus, majority), or how they should be structured. These issues are up to the elders, and the New Testament assumes that qualified elders who aspire to care for their church will organize themselves best according to the Holy Spirit's leading through the first among equals.

Therefore, local church elders must determine how to best organize themselves. Furthermore, how they organize themselves will change. For example, for many years the elder team of Mars Hill Church was only five men. As I write this book, though,

36. For example, 1 Timothy 3.

it is nearing thirty-six men. In the early years, the elders would meet in one room at my home, while our wives would meet for prayer and accountability in another room and our children all played together. At the end of our meetings we would all have dinner together as families. If we were to do that today, we would have a few hundred people in my home. We now have elder teams and not just an elder team, which means we have elder meetings and not just an elder meeting. The growth of our church and elder team has forced us to repeatedly rewrite our entire church bylaws, which explain how we organize ourselves.

For this kind of biblical faithfulness and practical flexibility to occur in a church there must be a distinction between principles and methods. The Bible is clear that God is to be worshiped, preaching is to occur, and the elders are to lead the church. However, the methods by which these can be done faithfully are many and must be culturally appropriated based upon where a church is ministering. As a result, things such as music styles, number of preachers, and how the elders are organized are freedoms that God allows the elders to decide, because God works through leaders empowered by his Spirit and governed by his Word under the rule of his living Son.

For people in the church, including leaders, this means that there must be a distinction between sin and style. Too many people respond to culturally appropriated style (e.g., music style, dress of the preacher, church décor) as if sins were being committed, when in fact methods of biblical principles are being implemented. This also means that the elders and other appointed leaders have the right to not only enforce God's rules of the Bible, but also have the freedom to make a few house rules as needed so that people know, for example, that they need to turn their phones off during a worship service or that members need to provide a giving pledge each year so that the church can make a reasonable budget projection.

A pastor is also blessed by having sheep, including fellow shepherds, who are not wrongly stiff-necked. Pastors need the people in their church to obey them and respect their God-given authority so that their work does not continually resemble a series of kicks to the groin.[37] As an elder in our church, I can say that being a pastor is both a high honor and a tremendous responsibility. I have found that the degree of joy in leading people is indeed inextricably connected to the willingness of those people to follow spiritual authority in a way that is not always without dissent, but is always with humble respect.

Lastly, spiritual authority that accompanies the office of elder can in no way be an excuse for overlooking sin or error of any kind. James 3:1 is clear that "Not many of you should become teachers, my brothers, for you know that we who teach will be judged with greater strictness." If it is believed that an elder is in sin, a formal charge should be brought according to the principles of 1 Timothy 5:19–21, which echoes Deuteronomy 19:15–19. Too often one disgruntled person who has a personal beef with the pastor and/or his wife becomes a source of gossip and rumor-mongering. However, personal matters are to be dealt with personally and not through gossip or false charges.[38] If the church does not follow a biblical process for church discipline, sin against a pastor is tolerated in the false name of accountability and making sure he is humble. Pastors must be held accountable for sin, but they must not be quickly accused or disciplined unless there are formal charges of sin that are investigated by the elders or a team they appoint on their behalf, and a verdict is rendered based upon credible evidence that a sin has been committed. Depending upon the severity of the offense, the elder may be rebuked publicly[39] or even removed from church leadership.[40]

37. Heb. 13:17; 1 Thess. 5:12–13.
38. Matt. 18:15–20.
39. 1 Tim. 5:19–21.
40. 1 Cor. 9:27.

The biblical differentiation between a sin that requires a rebuke and a sin that requires removal is important because all pastors are going to sin. But not all pastors are going to sin in a disqualifying way. If a pastor speaks harshly to his wife, for example, he should be held accountable, but, in most cases, this sin would not require a formal charge, unless such conduct was habitual or he was unrepentant. Instead, his wife or a close elder should approach the pastor—if he has not already repented due to the Holy Spirit's conviction. Thus, the accountability process for a pastor's non-disqualifying sin is to be dealt with in essentially the same manner as any "regular" (non-pastor-elder) Christian.

Lastly, to heed the Bible's warning against doing anything out of favoritism or partiality, sometimes an external team comprised of members of a church's denominational leadership or other godly pastors from the area are best suited to oversee the examination and trial of an elder charged with a disqualifying sin.

3

Women in Ministry

This chapter should include a wick because it is connected to a powder keg of controversial theological debates. Personally, I have found this issue to be among the most defining in my ministry. It seems that nearly every media piece ever done on me, for example, includes my position on women in ministry. This is because the gender issue in general, and women in ministry in particular, is a borderline that divides various groups. Where you land on this issue of women in ministry is in many ways a reflection of how you view Scripture, God, gender, marriage, and ministry. In an effort to be thorough, I will refer upon occasion to men's and women's roles in the home, as the family is the first ruling unit upon which the governments of church and state are built.

From Adam to Jesus

Not surprisingly, our study of the role of women in ministry must begin in Genesis, the book of beginnings, because God created male and female roles there with our first parents, Adam and Eve. Subsequently, those aspects of our humanity that are rooted in creation are binding upon people of all cultures and are not merely expressions of culture. This fact is important for our study of gender roles because throughout the New Testament, both Jesus[1] and Paul[2] commonly refer back to the Genesis creation account to clarify confusions that had arisen in their day regarding men's and women's

1. For example, Matthew 19:5 and Mark 10:7–8.
2. For example, Ephesians 5:31, 1 Timothy 2:14, and 1 Corinthians 11:7–9.

roles. Peter also refers to Genesis to straighten out confusion that had arisen over male and female roles in marriage.[3] We will likewise begin in the opening chapters of Genesis and follow their examples of beginning where the Bible does.

In Genesis 1:27–28 and 31, we discover that God made all that is. He made us male and female as the crowning jewel of his creation—not merely with the will of his Word, but rather with the loving work of his hand. This simple distinction is vital to our understanding of human nature because it undermines the popular social-psychology notions that there is no innate difference between males and females (except biology) and that gender tendencies are largely socially conditioned. God intentionally made us male and female, which means that males and females are in many ways quite different—a fact that parents with a son and a daughter have observed firsthand when their daughter holds her doll as her brother tries to shoot it with his hot dog.

In hearing that males and females are different, modern ears tuned by a culture of egalitarianism (meaning "equal" or "level") are prone to hear that males and females are not equal, which is untrue. The Bible teaches that both men and women are made in the image and likeness of God, which means that men and women are equal by virtue of creation. They do not need to be identical to prove their equality—in the same way that a right hand and left hand are different but equally necessary.

The image and likeness of God explains why human beings have dominion over lower creation, well-formed emotions, artistic creativity, complicated communication, social capacity, intellect, and a spirit that will live forever. God created men and women as his image-bearers upon the earth. Subsequently, since we are made male and female, it is clear that God's image and likeness is best shown forth by men and women who function together in partnership like the Trinity, in which God the Father,

3. 1 Pet. 3:1–7.

God the Son, and God the Spirit are equally God with distinctions, submission, and unity.

God made men and women with jobs to do, including having children and raising them to be fruitful upon the earth, ruling over creation, and creating a culture that honors the Lord. After creating the man and woman in his image and likeness and giving them their responsibilities, God said that all of this was "very good." Genesis 2 revisits the creation account with further details about the beginning of human history. We read in Genesis 2:18: "the Lord God said, 'It is not good that the man should be alone; I will make him a helper fit for him.'" There we find that although everything in Genesis 1 was declared "good" or "very good," there was one thing that was "not good"—that Adam was alone. This simple fact carries with it a number of important lessons.

First, Adam was made first as the head of all creation and bore primary responsibility for the creation that God had entrusted to him to steward. Likewise, in the New Testament we are repeatedly taught that men are to function as "heads" who take responsibility over their dominions of family[4] in the same way that Jesus is our ultimate Head who on the cross took responsibility for our sin, which was not his fault.[5] In Jesus' example we discover that when God made men to be heads, he was placing upon them the primary responsibility of leadership and service to ensure that all God had entrusted to their oversight (e.g., wives and children) would be well loved and cared for. To accomplish this high honor, men must learn to be like Jesus and take responsibility even when they are not at fault. Jesus' men should be about redeeming things that have been bent and stained by sin.

4. Eph. 5:23.
5. Col. 1:18; 2:10, 19; Eph. 1:10, 22; 4:15; 5:23.

Second, because God is a Trinity, men need a partner who is different from them but equal to them so that they can show forth the image and likeness of God.

Third, men need wives so utterly that, even though sin had not yet entered the world (and the world was technically perfect), it remained incomplete and therefore "not good" until the creation of Eve.

Fourth, men alone simply cannot be fruitful, multiply, honor God, and have the Trinitarian intimacy they were created to enjoy, and so God made women to be of help to men. Likewise, in 1 Corinthians 11:8–9 Paul says, "For man was not made from woman, but woman from man. Neither was man created for woman, but woman for man."

Clearly, God made women as helpers, which explains why it is not uncommon to find women pursuing careers and ministries that enable them to help other people; this is the reason they were made, and it is something in which they discover great satisfaction. While some modern women will undoubtedly bristle at the thought of being made as a helper, they should not, because they find themselves in good company with God, who is often referred to as our helper.[6]

The first encounter between a man and a woman is found in Genesis 2:22–25. There we read the first recorded words of any man as he sings a poetic love song to his bride on their wedding day. We also witness that the woman was taken from the side of the man, and that in the act of consummating their marriage, the two again become one flesh. Adam is given the honor of naming the opposite sex "woman." They enjoy the unity and joy that God intends for them to share. In this section of Scripture we also see that the overarching purpose God intends for husbands and wives is oneness, the same Hebrew word (*echad,* which means "many who are one") spoken three times daily by the ancient Jews in reference to the oneness of the Trini-

6. Pss. 10:14; 118:7; Rom. 8:26; Heb. 13:6.

tarian God in Deuteronomy 6:4. Lastly, we see that the family unit of the husband as leading head and the wife as lovely helper is the first governing unit upon which the governments of church and state are built.

Summarily, in the creation account of Genesis 1–2 we are given four reasons to believe that God made men with the patriarchal role of leadership upon the earth:

1. God made the man first, which established him as the leader responsible for the rest of creation in the same way that a firstborn son was responsible for his siblings throughout the Old Testament.
2. God intends that a wife be an equally valued helper alongside her husband and not a leader over him or a helper to any other man in the way she is to her husband, because they alone are "one flesh" in their covenant union. This is shown by the fact that the woman was taken from the side of the man as his equal.
3. God created the woman from the man, demonstrating her original dependence upon him as an ongoing pattern.
4. God permitted the man to name the woman and in that act exercise authority over her.

The creation account is a beautiful portrait of loving, unified harmony between men and women as they labor side by side as equals fulfilling the roles of leader and helper that God designed for them to fulfill. Tragically, the beauty of Genesis 1–2 is marred and stained by the sin of Genesis 3.

In addition to the man, the woman, and their God, a serpent enters the scene at the beginning of Genesis 3. In ancient literature the serpent was symbolic of chaos, and though this is a literal serpent, he indeed brings chaos into the otherwise perfect harmony of God's good creation. Echoing the book of beginnings, in Revelation (the book of endings) we discover that this serpent is none other than Satan himself.[7] This crafty liar[8] immediately attacks the truthfulness of God's Word with a subtle attempt to simply add a few details onto the commands God had given the man and woman.

In Eve's sin we witness the first attempt of a woman to usurp a man's role, with tragic results. Subsequently, it is important that we learn from her lesson and obey God's Word, rather than bend to the pressures we might face from our internal sinful desires and external cultural influences to mistrust God and do what seems best to us.

In Genesis 3 we also witness the passive cowardice of Adam, who stood idly by in silence, simply watching the Serpent lead his bride to disobey God. Like so many of his sons who have grievously followed in his lazy example, Adam actually watched his bride sin and then joined her in sin rather than doing anything to lovingly lead her back to the Lord.

We then witness their sin's effect—separation—as the man and woman cover their nakedness in mistrust and hide from God. However, God in his kindness pursued them as he has each of his children ever since. Curiously, however, though Eve sinned first, God called out rhetorically to Adam, "Where are you?" God held the man primarily responsible for the fall. In what has now become a common practice of men throughout history, Adam chose to blame God and the woman for the mess rather

7. Rev. 12:9; 20:2.
8. John 8:42–47.

than repent and take responsibility for his failure to lead as God had instructed him. Like many of her daughters since, Eve in effect defended her guilty husband, weakly attempting to blame Satan for all their troubles. As consequence for their sin, God pronounced a series of curses upon everyone involved.

Knowing that neither men nor women could possibly straighten out all they had made crooked, God promised Satan that a daughter of Eve (Mary) would one day give birth to a son (Jesus) who would be wounded by Satan in a conflict that would ultimately see Satan crushed in defeat. This curse upon Satan was fulfilled when Jesus Christ was exalted on the cross for the sins of his people,[9] and it will ultimately be completed when Jesus is exalted on his white throne to sentence the Serpent to the eternal torments of hell.[10]

God promised Eve that her domain of home would be cursed both in relation to her children and to her husband. First, becoming and being a mother would be a painful task. Second, she would be prone to mistrust her husband and, rather than follow his leadership, would continually seek to rule over him, though he would ultimately remain the leader in their relationship. Much ink has been spilled over what it means that Eve's desire would be to rule over her husband, but God graciously gave us a clear example in the next chapter (Genesis 4), where the exact same language of a woman's desire to rule over her husband is used for sin's desire to rule over Cain,[11] who ended up murdering his own brother Abel out of jealousy.

Since the day that this curse was pronounced, the gender wars have continually repeated the foolish loop of Genesis—cowardly men abdicate their responsibility to lead and women step up to fill the gap, with good intentions and tragic results. Today,

9. Col. 2:13–15.
10. Rev. 20:10.
11. Gen. 4:7.

a simple glance at the women's magazines on the rack at your local store verifies that women are still furiously trying to balance the overwhelming demands of motherhood (e.g., infertility, parenting) and marriage (e.g., singleness, marital conflict, divorce). God's intent was that through the pain and toil of trying to bring order into her home, the woman would be humbled and realize that she is just as unruly and complicated to govern for God (who is over her) as are her children (who are under her); this leads her to repentance before God for her sin of usurping her husband's position as family head and disobeying God's will for her.

God promised Adam that, because he listened to his wife when he should have spoken up for the Lord, the ground would be cursed under him. In this we see that the man's domain of marketplace has been cursed. No matter what job he labors at in an effort to provide for the needs of his family, his every effort will be met with resistance and complication, or what Genesis calls "thorns and thistles." Subsequently, both a man's wife and his job are perennial frustrations for him as they continually fail to follow his leadership, thus making his life toilsome. This also explains why the material for most stand-up comics and men's magazines revolves around how to get his woman and job in order, to no avail. As he cursed the woman, God cursed the man's dominion in an effort to humble him and cause him to experience what God does in relationship to the frustratingly disobedient man and bring him to repentance of sin and reliance on God's grace.

Genesis 3 then closes with Adam naming his wife "Eve," which means "giver of life," as every generation since has proceeded from this man and woman to experience the same frustrating gender conflicts. God then cast the man and woman from the garden of Eden and the tree of life because of his great love. After all, had we been permitted to partake of the tree of life, we would have lived forever as sinners separated from God, doing evil to one another upon the earth with no hope of a reprieve. We do not see the tree of life again until the closing chapter of Revelation when, following our resurrection, God's children enter into the new garden in heaven after the curse has been lifted and sin is no more.

Summarily, in Genesis 3 we discover three proofs (in addition to those found in Genesis 1–2) that further verify that God has created men for leadership and holds them responsible for their failures to lead well:

1. Though the woman sinned first, God held the man responsible, and when God came searching them out after their sin, he called out to the man.
2. The man was cursed for sitting idly by and listening to his wife when he should have taken the initiative to lead his family and speak against the lies of the Serpent.
3. The sin nature that all human beings possess from conception[12] is imputed to them through Adam and not Eve (though she sinned first), because as head of the human race he represented everyone in his sin.[13]

From Genesis 3 onward, human history is a tragic series of consequences for sin—as in Genesis 4 when Cain murders his brother Abel—and the sinful human heart sprints at breakneck speed into every sort of folly and death. But God's original intention that men be redeemed by God and participate with him in the work of redemption upon the earth remains. For example, in Genesis 5:1–2 we are told that God named the human race "man," or *adam* in Hebrew, as man is the head of mankind. Patriarchy

12. Pss. 51:5; 58:3.
13. Rom. 5:12–21; 1 Cor. 15:21–22.

remained the pattern throughout the Old Testament as the God of Abraham, Isaac, and Jacob was worshiped by families whose lineage was continually traced through the male line; this was recorded in books of the Bible, which were each penned by men. Throughout the world the creation order has been carried forth in every society. There is no evidence of any society ever being matriarchal (led by women). Simply, God's creation design of holding Adam and his sons primarily responsible for leadership and redemption remains intact until the coming of Jesus Christ, in fulfillment of the promise given to Eve.

From Jesus to Paul

During his life and ministry, Jesus treated women with great dignity and maintained the creation pattern of male leadership that permeated the Old Testament. Jesus clearly believed in Genesis 1:27, because he quoted it in Matthew 19:4 when he said, "he who created them from the beginning made them male and female."

In keeping with the Old Testament practice of reserving the senior leadership of God's people, the priesthood, exclusively for men, Jesus chose twelve men as his apostles. Some critics have argued that Jesus did not select female apostles because the culture in his day would not have accepted such a bold move. But they neglect to remember that Jesus' disciples were not chosen by chance or cultural acceptability but rather by the will of God the Father that was revealed to Jesus after spending a night in prayer over the matter.[14] It is doubtful that the people in Jesus' day would have been any more scandalized by the selection of a female disciple as they would have been over the selection of the traitor and extortionist, Matthew.

Furthermore, rather than obeying social customs, Jesus frequently broke them when he felt it was needed, and he was, in part, killed because of his violation of social

14. Luke 6:12–16.

customs. Examples include healing on the Sabbath,[15] throwing over tables in the temple,[16] eating with godless sinners,[17] and not washing his hands before eating.[18] Clearly, Jesus was no coward who bent to social pressure; if he had wanted to elevate women to the highest level of spiritual leadership he simply would have appointed them as apostles, which he did not.

Additionally, throughout his ministry Jesus often violated social taboos regarding women, as when he befriended the Samaritan women at the well of Sychar[19] and spoke publicly with the widow of Nain.[20] Jesus often healed and cast demons out of women.[21] Jesus used women as examples of exemplary faith in his teachings.[22] In what was likely quite controversial because women were generally omitted from theological instruction, Jesus did teach women theology.[23] Jesus allowed a sinful woman to anoint him.[24] Two of Jesus' closest friends were women whom he loved like sisters.[25] The funding of Jesus' ministry included generous support from godly women.[26] Lastly, the Bible records that godly women were the first to know that Jesus had risen from death.[27]

15. Mark 1:21–17.
16. John 2:14–17.
17. Matt. 9:11.
18. Mark 7:1–23.
19. John 4:7–26.
20. Luke 7:12–13.
21. Matt. 9:20–22; Luke 8:40–56; 13:10–17.
22. Matt. 25:1–10; Luke 4:26; 18:1–5; 21:1–4.
23. Luke 10:38–42; 23:27–31; John 20:10–18.
24. Luke 7:36–50.
25. Luke 10:38–39.
26. Luke 8:1–3.
27. Matt. 28:1–10.

In summary, Jesus honored, taught, and loved women and even included them in vital positions in his ministry. But he did not elevate women to the highest level of leadership, in keeping with the creation order and Old Testament precedent.

Following Jesus, the man God chose to most significantly shape the early church was Paul. Paul planted many of the early churches, wrote extensively on the leadership and organization of the early church, and pioneered the church's expansion into new cultures that had not yet heard about Jesus.

On one of his missionary journeys, Paul planted a church in the city of Ephesus.[28] Upon leaving for another mission, Paul gathered the senior leaders in the church—the elders—together to warn them that after his departure, false teachers would rise up from within the church, like Judas had among the disciples, and bring heresy and division unless they were sternly dealt with.[29] After his departure, Paul's prophecy came true as false teachers became very popular in the church, and so Paul commissioned his assistant Timothy to fight the heretics and command them to stop teaching false doctrines.[30] Paul commanded Timothy to not only quell this uprising, but also to replace it with "sound doctrine,"[31] which means doctrine that is healthy and that would cause the church and its members to be spiritually healthy and fruitful.

The heretics had apparently become very popular among young women who were forgoing modest dress, marriage, and motherhood to flaunt their freedom in Christ by dressing like tramps, gossiping, and trying to lead the charge of the church into culture clad with clear heels.[32] These women believed that they should abandon their feminine roles and instead occupy the positions of authority God intended for men

28. Acts 19.
29. Acts 20:13–38.
30. 1 Tim. 1:3–7, 18–20; 6:12, 20–21.
31. 1 Tim. 1:10.
32. 1 Tim. 2:9–3:2; 5:11–15; 2 Tim. 3:6–7.

to hold in the church. They were convinced of this error by the lies of the false teachers who said that Paul himself supported the idea of women occupying the highest position of leadership in the church, namely elder-pastor.

Thankfully, Paul wrote to the church to correct the heresy that was circulating regarding the role of women in ministry. (In this way, heretical false teachers are often a gift to the church because they force God's people to clarify sound doctrine.) The false feminist teachers in our own day who are promoting the same foolish nonsense that young women should embrace their sexuality and independence and forgo marriage and motherhood to pursue pastoral ministry would do well to simply listen to the words of Paul in 1 Timothy 2:11–3:5 and obey them.

1 Timothy 2:11–3:5

Let a woman learn quietly with all submissiveness. I do not permit a woman to teach or to exercise authority over a man; rather, she is to remain quiet. For Adam was formed first, then Eve; and Adam was not deceived, but the woman was deceived and became a transgressor. Yet she will be saved through childbearing—if they continue in faith and love and holiness, with self-control.

The saying is trustworthy: If anyone aspires to the office of overseer, he desires a noble task. Therefore an overseer must be above reproach, the husband of one wife, sober-minded, self-controlled, respectable, hospitable, able to teach, not a drunkard, not violent but gentle, not quarrelsome, not a lover of money. He must manage his own household well, with all dignity keeping his children submissive, for if someone does not know how to manage his own household, how will he care for God's church?

Paul begins by stating something quite controversial and unusual in his day—that women should learn theology. In our day, the application of this principle would mean that both men and women should be taught theology, be permitted to attend Bible college or seminary, and be encouraged to be theologically astute. Apparently the women in Ephesus were behaving in an unruly and disrespectful fashion during church services. They were much like their Christian sisters in Corinth,[33] whom Paul likewise commanded to be respectful toward church leadership. Paul also placed the onus for answering their many theological questions on their husbands as the heads of their homes. Paul added two requirements for the Ephesian women who wanted to learn theology: quietness and submission. Quietness here does not mean total silence, but rather a peaceable demeanor that is also required of men in Titus 2:2. The matter of women submitting to the pastoral leaders in the church directly correlates with the frequent command that women also submit to their husbands as the leaders in their homes.[34] Clearly, God's intention is that Christian women would be well-informed theologians, and to do so they must first learn to respect the male pastors whom God has appointed to instruct them.

While this simple admonition may appear patronizing to our modern ears, it is in fact because of this verse that it seems so. Ironically, if it were not for God's command through Paul that women be taught theology, modern-day feminist theologians would not be theologically astute enough to argue against the rest of Paul's teaching. After all, it is only in those places where Paul's influence has spread that women have been liberated, while throughout much of the rest of the world women are more likely to be considered mere property, denied an education, and handed a veil behind which to disappear into oblivion.

To correct the lies (which false teachers promulgated) that Paul approved of ministers in skirts, Paul emphatically commanded that women should not teach or have authority over men in the church. While Paul's command may seem straightforward enough to those willing to accept it, a wide variety of interpretive options has emerged.

33. 1 Cor. 14:33–35.
34. Eph. 5:21–33; Col. 3:18; Titus 2:3–5; 1 Pet. 3:1–6.

Those who hold a very liberal interpretation of Paul's command that women cannot teach or have authority over a man somehow mysteriously believe that he meant the exact opposite of what he said; they believe that women should teach and have authority over a man. However, despite the complex theological origami they subject this page of their Bibles to, if God wanted women to teach men and have authority over men, the Holy Spirit would have inspired Paul to simply say that, and not the direct opposite. Likewise, when the Bible elsewhere tells us not to kill innocent people, it does not mean that God wants us to kill innocent people, even if a "scholar" has more degrees than Fahrenheit, knows Greek, and published a book explaining it based upon drawings on the wall of a cave in upper Mesopotamia.

Those who hold a hard interpretation of Paul's command that women cannot teach or have authority over men in the church are prone to keep things tidy by simply telling women to only teach women and children (which is, admittedly, the cleanest place to draw the line). Those who hold a more flexible complementarian interpretation of Paul's commands (as I do) believe that the word used here for "authority" (the only place it is used in the New Testament) refers to the highest authority in the church, that of elder-pastor. This also seems logical in the context, as what immediately follows in the next chapter of 1 Timothy is the requirements for elders-pastors, which include being a mature Christian man and an exemplary husband and father. Correspondingly, Paul forbids women to teach (which would include preaching because it is an elder duty, according to 1 Timothy 5:17) and exercise authority (such as enforcing church discipline or setting doctrine) as elders-pastors. The teaching spoken of in 1 Timothy 5:17 likely refers to preaching and teaching as done by the elders, as every other time teaching is spoken of in the remainder of the letter it is in reference to the teaching of an elder.[35] The position I am arguing for is complementarian.

35. 1 Tim. 4:11; 5:7; 6:2.

A complementarian church should encourage women to use the spiritual gifts and natural abilities that God has given them to their fullest extent. This could be in anything from teaching a class to leading a Bible study, overseeing a ministry, leading as a deacon, speaking in church in a way that is not preaching, leading worship, serving communion, entering into full-time paid ministry as a member of the staff, and receiving formal theological education—or basically every opportunity in the church except what the Bible and the elders deem elder-only duties. Therefore, the issue is not if a woman can be in ministry, but rather what ministry a woman can be in and remain faithful to Scripture.

Chart 3.1 Women and Ministry: Three Views

Egalitarian (liberal)	Complementarian (moderate)	Hierarchical (conservative)
Men and women are partners together in every area of ministry. All ministries and offices in the church are open to men and women. Gender is not a relevant distinction for excluding any person from any church office.	Men and women are partners together in every area of ministry. All ministries in the church are open to all qualified men and women with the singular exception of the office of elder, which the Scriptures require to be a male-only office. Women can serve as deacons, teach, lead worship, serve communion, be in full-time paid ministry, etc.	Women and men are created to operate in different spheres of ministry within the church. Women are not permitted to be an elder or deacon, serve communion, teach men, lead worship, pray or speak in the church service, etc. Women should focus on building ministries for other women and children.

Again, some will try to find a way to evade the clarity of Paul's instruction that the role of elder-pastor, which is the position of senior leadership in the church, can be occupied solely by qualified men. One line of reasoning is that Paul was merely speaking of one church setting and that his instruction was not intended to be binding upon all churches. But 1 Timothy is a general epistle, which means it was intended to be applied to numerous churches throughout a large region. In fact, Paul says that it was intended for Christians "in every place."[36] There is no other declaration regarding who should lead the church that is nearly as comprehensive as the Pastoral Epistles (1 Timothy, 2 Timothy, and Titus), which unanimously teach that only qualified men should lead the church as elders-pastors. When this same issue is also addressed by Paul in 1 Corinthians 11, he ends his argument in verse 16 by saying, "If anyone is inclined to be contentious, we have no such practice, nor do the churches of God."

Another line of erroneous reasoning is that Paul did not select female elders-pastors because he was working within the confines of the culture of his day, and that had he lived today he would have chosen women because our culture would be more accepting of women as spiritual leaders. But Paul was frequently beaten for violating cultural norms of his day, such as ending the sacrificial system and not enforcing a host of Jewish cultural customs upon Gentile Christians, including circumcision, dietary restrictions, and festivals. Indeed, had Paul not so viciously undermined so many deeply valued cultural norms, he would have lived to a ripe old age instead of being beheaded by his angry critics.

Yet another line of false reasoning that attempts to open the pastorate to women is that women throughout the New Testament co-labored with Paul in vital ministry positions. This claim is indeed true and applies to such wonderful women as Priscilla, Lydia, Euodia, Syntyche, Phoebe, and many other godly women who served, led, and taught in the early church—but never as an elder-pastor. Of course, God gifts Christian women for fruitful lives of ministry that are desperately needed, but to jump from that to the premise that women should be elders-pastors violates the Bible's clear

36. 1 Tim. 2:8.

commands, examples, and precedents set forth by the male Old Testament priests and Jesus' male apostles.

While those who oppose Paul's clear teaching that only qualified men should be elders-pastors vary in the nuances of their arguments, at the heart of each is an insistence that male leadership in the governments of home and church are rooted in culture and not in creation. Therefore, they will purport that doctrine should change with culture rather than remaining constant. Again, the only problem with this position is the words of Paul in Scripture where he argues against female elders-pastors from the Genesis account of creation.[37] Whereas Paul's declaration that men should be pastors because God made them first may sound odd to us, it did make perfect sense to his original audience, who understood that throughout the Old Testament the firstborn was a position of extra responsibility in the family. Since God intentionally made man first, Paul reasons, then men are expected to take primary responsibility for the leadership of the church. Additionally, throughout the history of the Christian faith, this position has been widely agreed upon by everyone from the early church fathers John Chrysostom and Augustine to the Catholic theologian Erasmus to Lutheran reformer Martin Luther to Presbyterian reformer John Calvin to Baptist theologian John Gill and the Methodist founder John Wesley (who held the position until he had a change of mind later in life).

Paul further reasons that Eve was well intentioned in her attempt to function as the spiritual leader over the man, but was deceived or tricked by the Serpent.[38] Now, before you get all emotional and start blogging about me with big -ism words (e.g., sexism, chauvinism, patriarchalism, meanie-ism), please consider the content of the women's magazines at your local grocery store that encourage liberated women in

37. 1 Tim. 2:13.
38. 1 Tim. 2:14; 2 Cor. 11:3.

our day to watch porno with their boyfriends, master oral sex for men who have no intention of marrying them, pay for their own dates in the name of equality, spend an average of three-fourths of their childbearing years having sex but trying not to get pregnant, and abort one-third of all babies—and ask yourself if deception does not have a nice ring to it?

The women in Ephesus had apparently been duped into the same folly as modern-day women, as they dressed like tramps[39] and happily had sex without seeking marriage.[40] So Paul lovingly liberates such "liberated" women from their "liberation" by encouraging them to return to the role that God had created them for, namely being happy as faithful Christians serving God according to their gifts and not despising the noble roles of wife and mother.[41]

Tragically, our day is filled with women who, like their mother Eve, have been deceived so thoroughly that they regard marriage and motherhood as denigration rather than an honor. They think that unless someone calls you "pastor," you are a junior varsity Christian, which is silly when you stop to consider that the vast majority of the men in any church aren't pastors either. Thankfully, Paul loves women enough that he commands Christian men to take responsibility for their homes and churches.

The February 2004 cover story "Where Are the Women?" of *Fast Company* magazine reported that, despite enormous efforts from the feminist movement to remove women from their homes, marriages, and motherhood and instead raise them to the highest levels of the corporate world, their aspirations have been unmet. Why? The non-Christian article reports that women want to be wives and mothers, and that no

39. 1 Tim. 2:9.
40. 1 Tim. 5:11–15.
41. 1 Tim. 2:15.

matter how much money they are offered, they are reticent to work the number of hours required to lead a large company because to do so would mean they would have to forgo marriage and motherhood. In retrospect, perhaps God's creation order has remained more intact than one would imagine in light of the pounding it has taken.

From Paul to Us

Practically, the Adam and Eve paradigm of weak, aloof men and well-intentioned, deceived women trying to make up for their lack is again normative in our day. In a March 6, 2000, article titled "Women Are the Backbone of the Christian Congregations in America," researcher George Barna reported how the sons of Adam and daughters of Eve are faring in our present day:

- Over 90 percent of Protestant pastors and 100 percent of Catholic pastors are male.
- The American population is roughly 50 percent male and 50 percent female.
- 60 percent of American Christians are female.
- There are between 11 and 13 million more American Christian women than men.
- 46 percent of American women say they are born again, compared to 36 percent of American men.
- Christian women are 100 percent more likely than men to be in a discipleship process.
- Christian women are 56 percent more likely than men to be in non-pastoral church leadership.
- Christian women are 54 percent more likely than men to be in a small group.

- Christian women are 46 percent more likely than men to disciple others.
- Christian women are 39 percent more likely than men to have a devotional time.
- Christian women are 34 percent more likely than men to volunteer for a church.
- Christian women are 29 percent more likely than men to read the Bible in a week.
- Christian women are 29 percent more likely than men to attend church in a week.
- Christian women are 29 percent more likely than men to share their faith in a year.
- Christian women are 23 percent more likely than men to donate money to a church monthly.
- Christian women are 16 percent more likely than men to pray in a week.

Clearly, the pattern set forth by Adam and Eve of men abandoning their responsibility to lovingly lead their homes and churches, coupled with well-intentioned but deceived women stepping in to fill the holes, is still being followed in our day. Subsequently, one of the greatest needs that the Christian church in general must face is its inability to attract, convert, train, and inspire men to lovingly and responsibly lead like Jesus.

A complementarian church must focus intently on raising up men, particularly young men, to be responsible, loving leaders in their families and churches like Jesus and unlike Adam. Simply, one of the kindest things we can do for women and children is to raise up men who are good Christians, husbands, fathers, and Christian brothers. This point was humorously made to me after one of our evening services during a conversation with a younger female pastor from another church. She told me that she very much enjoyed frequently attending our church but was very disappointed that we did not have women pastors. When I asked her why she would regularly visit our church in the evening after leading at her own church in the morning if she did not like our leaders, she blushed and tried to avoid the question. When I pressed her for an honest response, ironically she admitted that she was single and wanted to be married and have children but there were no good men in her church; she attended Mars Hill because she admired the quality of a few thousand young single men and hoped to find a husband in their midst while complaining that we should be more like her church.

I realize that some people who disagree with me on the matter of women as elders-pastors are still Christians with whom I will spend eternity in heaven. While our biblical convictions on this matter run very deep at our church and are not up for debate, we will welcome into our church and church membership Christians who can obey Paul's command to the women in Ephesus that they come with minds willing to learn and with peaceable hearts not intent on arguing or disrespecting the leadership of the church elders. As leaders, we seek to lovingly instruct both men and women in their God-ordained, equal and complementary gender roles so that they can experience the joy and fulfillment that only comes through humble obedience to God.

4

Deacons

It did not take long for the senior leaders in the early church to become overextended, too distracted, and ineffective. In Acts 6:1–7 we learn that the apostles became overburdened with the mercy ministry of caring for needy widows, which resulted in a racist neglect of non-Hebrew widows while the Hebrews were being favored. Apparently, the apostles were willing to do the work of feeding widows but were not particularly adept at it, and they were torn between that need and their other pastoral duties, particularly prayer and Bible study. Therefore, it was decided that the apostles would appoint pastoral assistants to care for the widows, thereby enabling the apostles to focus on prayer and Scripture.

Because this section of Scripture is descriptive and not prescriptive (it tells us what happened but does not tell us exactly what we should do) and does not explicitly mention deacons, we must be careful not to read too much into the text. For example, seven men were appointed to feed Grecian widows, but that does not mean that a local church is in sin if it does not appoint exactly seven men to make sandwiches for Grecian widows. But from this section of Scripture we can extract the biblical principle that when senior spiritual leadership is overburdened to the degree that they do not have time for prayer, Bible study, and the care of needy people, they are free to appoint pastoral assistants to help alleviate some of their burden.

This simple pattern of senior leaders doing a work until it becomes too large and burdensome for them to continue is the pattern of the New Testament—elders are continually appointed first in local churches, and once they are overburdened then they appoint pastoral assistants to aid them. These pastoral assistants are called "deacons." They are mentioned on two occasions in the New Testament. Both occasions are in relation to elders because the two groups of leaders work so closely together.[1] Practically, elders and deacons work together like left and right hands, with elders specializing in leading by their words and deacons specializing in leading by their works.

Deacons are the servants of the church who are also qualified for the ministry of overseeing and caring for God's people by qualifications that are nearly identical to the elders—minus the teaching and preaching abilities. They must have theological convictions that are true to Scripture.[2] Deacons occupy the second-highest position of leadership in the church, and serve as helpers to the elders in a manner similar to how wives serve in the home alongside their husbands who lead the family. Deacons are appointed only after they have proven themselves to the elders as faithful and mature church members.[3]

1 Timothy 3:8–13

Deacons likewise must be dignified, not double-tongued, not addicted to much wine, not greedy for dishonest gain. They must hold the mystery of the faith with a clear conscience. And let them also be tested first; then let them serve as deacons if they prove themselves blameless. Their wives likewise must be dignified, not slanderers, but sober-minded, faithful in all things. Let deacons each be the husband of one wife, managing their children and their own households well. For those who serve well as deacons gain a good standing for themselves and also great confidence in the faith that is in Christ Jesus.

1. Phil. 1:1; 1 Tim. 3:1–13.
2. 1 Tim. 3:9.
3. 1 Tim. 3:10.

Twelve Requirements and Two Rewards of a Deacon from 1 Timothy 3:8–13

1. Dignified: worthy of respect, without any character defect, holy
2. Not double-tongued: sincere, heartfelt, earnest, honest, authentic
3. Not addicted to much wine: without addictions, self-controlled
4. Not greedy for dishonest gain: not a lover of money, financially content and upright
5. Hold the mystery of the faith with a clear conscience: sound biblical theology held with deep conviction
6. Tested: proven worthy over time

Additional Requirements for Female Deacons

7. Dignified: honored by both men and women as exemplary Christians, without any character defect
8. Not slanderers: not malicious talkers, not prone to sins of the tongue such as gossip, slander, lying, etc.
9. Sober-minded: temperate, not prone to emotionalism
10. Faithful in all things: trustworthy in everything, faithful in all life roles (e.g., wife, mother, daughter, sister)

Additional Requirements for Male Deacons

11. Husband of one wife: a one-woman man, sexually pure
12. Manages his children and household well: godly husband and father who leads, manages, and provides for his family

Rewards for Faithful Deacons

1. A good standing for themselves: honored and respected by God's people in the church

2. Great confidence in the faith: assurance in their faith, a deep confidence in the power of the gospel and the security of their relationship with God

While the duties of an elder are clearly articulated throughout the New Testament, the same cannot be said for the duties of deacons. The Greek word for "deacon" simply means "servant," and beyond that title we are given little indication of what a deacon should do. This is because while the duties of an elder are universally constant in every church in every place in every age, the duties of deacons vary according to the needs of local churches and their elders. In this way, the Bible brilliantly establishes a theologically grounded, morally qualified group of senior elder leaders, and grants them the freedom to appoint whatever deacons are needed to help them lead the church, in whatever areas they deem require a deacon to lead. From the qualifications, we can infer that deacons will generally be handling church money, managing church systems, and meeting mercy needs, and that they will be privy to the most intimate details of people's lives.

Female Deacons

There is some dispute as to whether or not a woman can be a deacon. Much of this debate centers around Paul's qualifications for deacons in 1 Timothy 3:11: "Their wives [or *Wives*, or *Women*] likewise must be dignified, not slanderers, but sober-minded, faithful in all things." Paul's language in the original Greek of this verse is, admittedly, complicated. In regards to the meaning of this verse, there are essentially three possibilities: (1) Paul may be speaking of women who assist deacons; (2) Paul may be speaking of women who are the wives of male deacons (However, if the verse is speaking of qualifications for male deacons' wives then we have a problem because there is no similar requirement for the wives of male elders. This would mean that male deacons have a higher standard to meet than male elders, who hold the highest position of authority in the church. Therefore, the verse cannot logically be accepted as an additional requirement for the wives of male deacons.) (3) Paul may be speaking of women who are deacons. Various translations opt for one of these three interpretations and often include a footnote that explains the other options, as the translators are also unsure exactly what is meant. Additionally, some translations (such as the New International Version and the English Standard Version) translate the word for "woman" as "wives," which adds to the confusion.

At Mars Hill Church, we believe that the verse can and does mean all three things. Indeed, we believe the Bible teaches here that a woman can be a deacon, that some female deacons are married to male deacons (as is often the case at our church), and that some female deacons will also be assisting other male deacons. If understood this way, the text flows quite nicely as the requirements of 1 Timothy 3:8–10 are for both male and female deacons—indicated by the word "likewise" in the following verse (3:11), which thus applies those qualifications to women. Verse 11 goes on to list the additional requirements for female deacons, while verses 12–13 list the additional requirements for male deacons. Practically, this also makes sense, as Paul is indicating that a male deacon is most vulnerable to sexual sins, while a female deacon is most vulnerable to emotional and verbal sins; women who are prone to disagree with his words merely prove his point.

Those who oppose the appointment of female deacons usually do so by stating that Paul had just previously forbidden women from teaching or having authority over a man (1 Tim. 2:12). But in that verse the word Paul uses for "authority" is a special word used only on this one occasion in the Bible, which means he was speaking of a special authority. The teaching he refers to is in reference to the teaching or preaching done during the gathered worship service of the church, which is clearly reserved for the male elders.[4] Women are permitted to teach in contexts that are not related to the position of elder.[5] Therefore, Paul does not forbid a woman from all teaching and all authority, but rather he forbids them from teaching and ruling as an elder. Again, this interpretation of 1 Timothy 2:12 also fits the context of the verse nicely, as the verses which follow it further define the qualifications of an elder.

Further evidence for women deacons is found in Romans 16:1 where Phoebe is greeted first, which denotes honor; she is also called a servant, which is the same word for deacon and likely indicates she was a deacon. Additionally, other women whom Paul honors for their assistance to him may also have been female deacons. Among them are Mary,[6] Tryphena and Tryphosa,[7] and Euodia and Syntyche.[8] Lastly, every church does have women in positions of leadership, even if their roles are restricted to administration, women's ministries, and children's ministries. Unless a church calls such women by the biblical title of "deacon" and holds them accountable to the biblical qualifications for their leadership, they are forced to invent titles like director and such. This is problematic because it has no biblical precedent. Therefore, at Mars Hill Church, we have only male elders who are the senior leadership in the church, and we appoint both male and female deacons as assistant leaders in the church in the same way that a wife is an assistant leader and helper to her husband in the home.

In closing, I am deeply grateful for the army of male and female deacons who humbly serve and are in every way a vital complement to the work of our elders.

4. 1 Tim. 5:17.
5. For example, Titus 2:3–5.
6. Rom. 16:6.
7. Rom. 16:12.
8. Phil. 4:2–3.

Among them is a woman named Crystal who is my research and editing deacon. Because of her gifts I am able to write books such as this one. Without the gifts and service of people like her, our church simply fails to be what Jesus intends for it to be and ceases to do what Jesus intends for it to do. That being said, we will now examine church members who work as leaders with the elders and deacons to accomplish Jesus' mission for a church in a culture.

5

Members

In addition to elders and deacons who lead the local church are non-Christians who are in the process of sorting out their relationship with God and church members who call the church their home and take responsibility to ensure its health and growth. Church members are Christians whose eyes are capable of seeing beyond their own navels. They realize that God died not just for them but for their church.[1] They also realize that he commands them to selflessly give of their money[2] and abilities in order to build up their church.[3]

Some Christians question whether or not they need to have a church home in which they participate as official members. But the illustrative imagery of the church throughout the New Testament includes the fact that Christians are to work together like a family[4] or as the parts of a body.[5] The early church had a notion of membership that included numerical record,[6] records of widows,[7] elections,[8] discipline,[9] account-

1. Acts 20:28.
2. 2 Cor. 8–9.
3. 1 Cor. 14:12.
4. 1 Tim. 3:15; 5:1–2.
5. 1 Cor. 12:16–17.
6. Acts 2:37–47.
7. 1 Tim. 5:3–16.
8. Acts 6:1–6.
9. Matt. 18:15–20; 1 Corinthians 5; Gal. 6:1.

ability,[10] and an awareness of who was a church member.[11] At the risk of stating the obvious, to obey most of the New Testament teaching requires that a Christian be a member of a local church, since most of the epistles open by saying "to the church."[12]

Therefore, church members are, in a sense, leaders of the church who serve according to their abilities in accordance with Jesus' command to love God and their neighbor; this shows up not just in what they feel, but in what they do. The church members must be trained and released to use their spiritual gifts in various ways so that they too are leading the church behind the elders and deacons as the priesthood of believers that Scripture speaks of throughout the New Testament. This includes nursery captains working with the little people, home-based Bible study leaders, worship band leaders, usher and greeter captains, technical team leaders, and leaders of various mercy ministries. Those who function as exemplary church members are then qualified to occupy the church leadership positions of deacon and elder, respectively.

To become a member at Mars Hill, one must be a Christian who has met the requirements of membership established by our elders. These include being baptized at some point as a demonstration that Jesus died and rose to wash them from sin. Members must also complete the Doctrine Series, which explains the essential beliefs of Christianity and our church, and sign a written covenant[13] with the elders to do such things as serve in the church, pray for the church, give to the church, read their Bible regularly, pray, attend church services, and share the gospel with others in word and deed.

10. Heb. 13:17.
11. Rom. 16:1–16.
12. 1 Cor. 1:2; 2 Cor. 1:1; Gal. 1:2; Eph. 1:2; Phil. 1:1; 1 Thess. 1:1; 2 Thess. 1:1; Rev. 1:4.
13. A copy of this covenant is in Appendix 3.

Those people who become church members then meet with deacons or other church leaders who explain how to navigate through the systems in our church. The deacons also help them determine which area of ministry they are best suited to serve in and how to begin a new ministry if they have a good idea that the church needs to implement.

Our members also fill out an annual financial pledge, and we send out quarterly giving updates to each member. Their pledges help us to set our annual budget based on a credible estimate of what our income will be for that year. Pledges also help our members to have a plan as faithful stewards. Our church members provide the majority of financial support and volunteer hours; without them we simply could not operate.

Our members are also given some privileges that we do not extend to other people in general. For example, we have an online network called The City where the people of our church share goods and prayer requests, ask questions, and build community online. Though it is open to both members and guests, members have greater access to The City. We also operate an "open books" policy for church members and are happy to answer reasonable questions they may have about financial church matters.

Additionally, only members are allowed to oversee certain areas of ministry, such as children's ministry, worship bands, finances, and teaching. Non-members are intentionally encouraged to serve throughout the church as a connecting point for community and for the gospel. This is important so that our church can act missionally by bringing people, including non-Christians, into active participation in the life of the church with the intent of seeing lost people become Christians and disconnected Christians become vitally connected to the church ministries and members and eventually become faithful church members themselves.

As a general rule, between one-third and one-half of a healthy, growing church's total weekly attendance should be church members. If that number becomes too small, then the leadership pipeline is drying up, the church is not growing, or new people are somehow not becoming members of the church family, and the members who are serving will quickly burn out. Conversely, if that number becomes too large, then there could be a lot of dead weight in the church, and the leaders need to get rid of "members" who do not participate in worship regularly, give, serve, or follow through on whatever additional requirements they agreed to when they became members.

Leadership Teams

From God existing as a Trinitarian community to Jesus sending his own disciples out in teams, the message of the Bible from Genesis to Revelation is that unified teams are the best way to do ministry. Therefore, in this section we will explore how to build unified leadership teams.

First, unity is incredibly important if the mission of the church to glorify God in heaven and reach people on earth is to be fulfilled. The church follows the leadership for better or for worse—whether or not the leadership itself is unified. Unity is gained slowly and lost quickly and therefore must be labored for continually. Unity is so important that Jesus often prayed for it and Paul repeatedly commands it.[1]

Second, unity must be defined because people have varied ideas of what it means to lead a church or ministry in unity. Unity must include theological agreement about what doctrines you will and will not fight over, relational warmth and sincere friendships that include spouses and children, philosophical agreement regarding what ministry methods will and will not be used, and a missional partnership that agrees to stay on task to fulfill God's mission for that church or ministry in that culture. We will now examine some very practical ways to help build and maintain unity.

Act Your Size

The number of leadership teams and the complexity of their makeup will increase exponentially as a church grows larger. Simply, a bigger church has more ministries,

1. 1 Cor. 1:10; 2 Cor. 13:11; Eph. 4:3; Phil. 1:27.

more people, more leaders, more teams, and more complexity. Therefore, a larger church must not expect decisions to be made in the same way as a smaller church, and a smaller church wanting to grow must change the way its leaders make decisions so that it can grow larger. Chart 6.1 summarizing various church sizes illustrates this point; as you will see, the various plateau points where churches stop growing are points where leaders must make changes if there are to be more people worshiping Jesus at that church (which is ultimately the one question that answers all others).

The rough breakdown of church sizes in America is as follows, based on my research. No one is exactly sure how many non-Catholic Protestant churches there are in the United States, but the general figures are somewhere between four hundred thousand and five hundred thousand churches. So, for purposes of this rough estimate, I am assuming that there are four hundred thousand non-Catholic Protestant churches in the United States. I am also assuming that the reported attendance at these churches is accurate, something that is highly questionable since over-reporting of church attendance is estimated by some to be as high as fifty percent.[2] A rough estimate of weekly church attendance for adults and children in America breaks down as follows:

Larger churches have fewer people making decisions than smaller churches, multiple leadership teams instead of one or a few, and specialized leaders (whereas smaller churches have leaders who are generalists working in multiple areas). Larger churches also have to plan their calendar out further than smaller churches because they are dealing with more people and complexity, which requires more foresight. Part of this includes knowing what game you are playing.

2. For example, see Robert D. Putnam, *Bowling Alone* (New York: Simon and Schuster, 2000), 71; and also, David T. Olson, *Ten Fascinating Facts about the American Church*, CD-ROM, slide 3, The American Church, www.TheAmericanChurch.org.

Chart 6.1 *Church Attendance in America*

Weekly Church Attendance	Number of Churches in America	Percentage of All Churches in America
45 people or fewer	100,000	25 percent
75 people or fewer	200,000	50 percent
150 people or fewer	300,000	75 percent
350 people or fewer	380,000	95 percent
800 people or fewer	392,000	98 percent
800 people or more	8,000	2 percent
2,000 people or more	870	0.22 percent
3,000 people or more	425	0.11 percent
6,000 people or more	100	0.025 percent
10,000 people or more	40	0.01 percent

Know What Game You Are Playing

Churches do not merely grow, they also change. While many people want growth, they do not want change, which leads to frustration that can result in conflict. My friend Pastor Larry Osborne has been very helpful in my understanding of some of the practical changes that occur as a church grows; here I summarize many of the points from his book *The Unity Factor*, along with many personal conversations we have had over the years.[3]

His basic point is that as a church grows so does the game the leaders are playing. In a small church, the first-among-equals pastor is essentially a solo decathlete who does a bit of preaching, administration, building maintenance, bookkeeping, bulletin copying, wedding officiating, hospital visiting, and Bible study teaching. In

3. Larry W. Osborne, *The Unity Factor* (Vista, CA: Owl's Nest, 2001).

a medium-sized church, the leadership team grows and becomes more like a golf game, where the first among equals and a few of his buddies who are fellow elders interact informally over meals and such and have a warm community in which they make decisions together. As the leadership team grows in a larger church, it becomes more like a basketball team where things are more formalized, the first-among-equals pastor functions like the point guard running all the plays, and the other elders have positions they are playing with specialized areas of ministry oversight. In those churches that become very large, the game changes entirely and is more like a football team, which is really multiple teams (e.g., offense, defense, special teams) with teams within the teams (e.g., receivers, linemen, running backs, line-backers, cornerbacks, kickers, kick returners), each with separate coaches and separate practices.

The threat to unity in a church comes when the leaders and teams do not know and accept what game they are playing. The game has clearly changed when the leadership team grows; this can lead to pain points such as increased miscommuni-cation, burnout, things starting to fall through the cracks, people starting to jockey for power and money and making threatening demands, leaders beginning to feel out of the information loop, and conflict arising over who makes what decisions. When these pain points arise, the tendency is for everyone to run to the first-among-equals elder and demand that they be kept in close relational proximity to him and his family so that they are not displaced from power. However, this leads to the first-among-equals pastor being crushed under conflicting demands and relational overload that threaten to destroy him. What the various leaders and teams do not realize is that not all leaders in the church can be buddies issued matching sweatshirts with the first-among-equals pastor and his wife. As the number of team members grows, the lines of communication become increasingly complex, taxing, and exhausting:

- 2 People = 2 lines of communication
- 3 People = 6 lines of communication
- 4 People = 12 lines of communication
- 6 People = 30 lines of communication

In this very tenuous season of game-changing for leaders, they have only two options. First, the teams can accept the new game and play it so that as many people as possible worship Jesus. Second, the teams can try to play the new game by the old rules until the first-among-equals pastor either burns out or serious conflict arises and, after some bloody church fights, the church shrinks back down to the size that the old game of leadership can manage; this option ensures that not everyone who could have worshiped Jesus does because the leaders acted for their personal comfort and not for Christ.

Church leaders and their teams that refuse to act their size and play whatever game leads to the most people possible worshiping Jesus are in sin and need to practice repentance. That repentance includes building as many teams as needed to get the job done, providing enough layers of authority to oversee various teams as needed, ceasing excessive relational demands on the senior leader(s) and their families, and being willing to accept that some leaders who really like the old game will not be at the highest levels of the church and may need to leave the church altogether to work somewhere else where the size is more suited to their degree of giftedness and personal preference. Those who remain in the church and are willing to play the game God has given them and act the size to which Jesus has called them then need to be broken into three kinds of teams, which we will now explore. As a practical aside, these teams cannot become too large or the same pain points I described above show up yet again. I have found that, for some reason, teams of three to seven people seem to function best.

Additionally, there always needs to be clarification about the chain of command for communication and decision-making. If the chain of command is not respected, then the senior leader is bombarded by requests from every level of the church and gets pulled into way too many management details that other leaders should take responsibility for. Furthermore, to guard the chain of command, the senior leader must also work through that same chain when speaking into issues of leadership and management in the church. By this he will empower and respect the spiritual authorities in place throughout varying levels of the church's leadership structure. The most likely people to understand the need for the chain of command are the kings, whereas the priests are the least likely to understand this need. We will now explore the roles of prophets, priests, and kings in the church.

Prophets, Priests, and Kings

We began by establishing that Jesus Christ is the Senior Pastor/Chief Shepherd in the church. We have established that the other leaders, such as elders, deacons, and members, are to follow and emulate Jesus Christ. What we have yet to clearly and theologically distinguish are the various ways in which Jesus leads and ministers in the church.

This insight has been a great help to our church, thanks to some ongoing conversations with Pastor David Fairchild, who is part of our Acts 29 Church Planting Network and a dear friend. Within the Reformed theological tradition of which I am a part, there is a long history of seeing Jesus in his three offices of Prophet, Priest, and King. These are mega-themes of Scripture connected to Jesus from Genesis to Revelation. As Prophet, Jesus preached and taught Scripture with authority. As Priest, Jesus cares for people and deals with their sin compassionately. As King, Jesus demonstrated his rule over creation through miracles while on the earth, and today rules and reigns over his people through church leaders, principles, and systems by the Holy Spirit and according to his Word.

As leaders who are flawed and not Jesus Christ, we are an imperfect combination of these three roles and tend to be strongest in one or two of the three. Rarely does someone have a high capacity in every area.

Prophets tend to be strong at vision, study, preaching, teaching, doctrinal truth, refuting error, and calling people to repent of sin. Their weakness is that without kingly help, the crowd they gather is never mobilized for mission, and without priestly help, they and their teaching can become cold, impersonal, legalistic, and impractical. In short, prophets like to correct doctrinal error and call people to repent of sin and obey Scripture.

Priests have a deep understanding of human suffering and are compassionate and merciful in tending to the needs of hurting people so that they are loved to spiritual maturity. Priests are masters at resolving conflicts between people so that there is reconciliation through the gospel. The weakness of priests is that they are so people-focused that they tend to be disorganized. Without kingly help, they run from crisis to crisis without building other leaders and systems to care for people in large numbers. Without prophetic support, they can be merciful and patient to the point of enabling people in their sin and not calling them to an urgent repentance. In short, priests like caring for hurting people.

Kings excel at systems, policies, procedures, planning, team building, mission executing, and simply maximizing resources to accomplish measurable results. Without prophetic support, a king can lead people into false doctrine and mere pragmatism. Without priestly support, a king can burn his people out and use them for tasks without truly caring for them and seeking their spiritual growth. In short, kings like charts, graphs, and checking things off from their to-do list.

In every church, there must be a variety of teams focused on specific ministry needs in the areas of prophetic, priestly, and kingly ministry. These teams are best served by a combination of gifts so that the leadership teams are biblically solid (prophet), grace centered (priest), and actually get the job done (king). If not, conflict can arise between these three various types of leaders. We have found through painful trial and error that ultimately large ministry areas must be led by a king in the first-among-equals position for that team if there is any hope of anything getting done well. Too often churches that have their people nominate their team leaders see only the priests elected to first-among-equals status because they love well, but in the end they also thwart the ability of the church and its ministries to flourish because they fail to build a kingdom in which as many people as possible are reached and loved well. Lastly, as someone who has bits of all three but is first a prophet, then a king, and lastly a priest, my experience has shown that priests often question the rule of kings and prophets because they seem to be less concerned about people when the truth is that prophets, kings, and priests each love Jesus and people but simply love them in different ways through teaching, organizing, and shepherding, respectively. Once these differentiations are understood, the teams are then able to be deployed to either the air war or ground war.

Air War and Ground War

In our church, I often distinguish between what I call the air war and the ground war.

The air war includes such things as preaching and teaching at gathered church services and other large events such as church-based conferences, retreats, and training events. The air war at our church also includes our Web site, vodcasts and podcasts, and publishing.

Chart 6.2 *Air War vs. Ground War*

Air War	Ground War
Leads the mission	Follows the air war
Has a primary visible leader	Has multiple, less-visible leaders
Requires prophets and kings	Requires priests and kings
Deals with the masses	Deals with individuals and small groups
Is event centered	Is relationship centered
Is the church's front door	Is the church's living room
Draws people to the church	Connects people to the church
Proclaims with authority	Explains with accountability
Provides general principles	Provides personal applications

The ground war includes such things as home-based Bible studies, smaller training classes, individual counseling appointments, and recovery groups for addictions and sexual abuse.

In my experience, most church leaders are good at either the air war or the ground war. For a church to succeed, though, it must have both an air war and a ground war. A church with only an air war will have large Sunday meetings but will not see the kind of life transformation in people that can only come through the intense efforts of a well-organized ground war. Such churches give the appearance of health because of their sheer size, but that is often nothing more than an illusion. This is sometimes even tragically made visible by the moral failure of a senior leader who needed more ground war in his own life as well as his church.

Conversely, a church with only a ground war may have mature people but does not grow or see new converts meeting Jesus regularly. Despite their crummy band and a preacher who is as clear and compelling as the teacher from the *Peanuts* cartoons, he's a really nice guy who loves everyone to the degree that they will endure Sunday services.

Sadly, both kinds of churches tend to become very proud and defensive about their strengths while neglecting their glaring weaknesses. Therefore, a church must not only have unified teams with multiple leaders operating in prophetic, priestly, and kingly ways, but it must also have a good air war and a good ground war. The air war is where the prophets excel and the ground war is where the priests excel. The only way both can work together in harmony is if the kings ensure that things are organized. The kings pull the air and ground wars together in such a way that there is unity between their respective teams and a mutual respect and appreciation for the work of the other. For this to occur there must also be a distinction between the leadership offices and the leadership courts.

Offices and Courts

Not only must a church have biblically qualified leaders holding biblical offices, there must also be a clear understanding of various courts of leaders that make various decisions so that there is not confusion and conflict. The offices represent the individual people and their roles, while the courts represent decision-making teams with a defined authority and responsibility.

As an example, there was a day when the elders of our church served as a singular court and could vote and render verdicts on various issues in the church. At the time I am writing this book, though, we are expanding from three campuses to six campuses and from seven services to at least sixteen services scattered throughout the entire region surrounding Seattle. We now have nearly one hundred employees along with two thousand church members and are trying to grow the church from six thousand to ten thousand people. Obviously, the thirty-two elders cannot meet to vote on every ministry decision.

While this example may be extreme, the only way we were able to get to this point of organizational complexity was by continually redefining our courts and their decision-making authority. Some of the biggest fights in a church occur over which courts get to make which decisions and who does not have the authority to make which decisions. So much of what I have written in this book can only be implemented effectively if the proper verdict-rendering courts are established so that conflict and chaos cannot rise up to sidetrack reorganization and repentance in those churches that need it. This begins with a clear understanding of the specific roles each leader assumes with unity and humility so they can lead the church in a way that follows Jesus, is faithful to Scripture, and is fruitfully on mission in culture.

Fight like Family

Everything I have written about in this chapter is necessary for a church to grow. Growth is good because the more people who worship Jesus the better. However, churches often do not pursue growth for one of two reasons. One, they pridefully ascribe a moral value to a certain church size and refuse to grow beyond that size because being whatever size they feel is holy makes them holy, which is nonsense and unholy logic. Two, they don't like to fight. The truth is that growth comes at a price because:

1. Growth causes change.
2. Change causes complexity.
3. Complexity causes concern.
4. Concern causes conflict.

In conclusion, implementing anything from this chapter so that your church can be healthy and grow like healthy things are supposed to will require change. This means that no matter what, there will be conflict. Rather than avoiding conflict with people to instead have conflict with Jesus for failing to do what he tells you to, you will just need to accept that a good church fight is bound to happen if you want to change things. The key is to always remember that the church is a family, and so we fight with one another like every good family does, not as enemies, but knowing that we love each other.

My final word in this book is to encourage those of you who are in churches that were once on mission but have become museums that exist to remember the past rather than pursue the future to humbly work for biblical repentance, knowing that a long-overdue, sanctified church fight might ensue to God's glory.

Appendix 1

Answers to Common Questions about Church Leadership

What Can I Do if I Want to Plant a Church?

Log on to www.acts29network.org to find information about our church planting network and resources to help you decide if God has called you to plant a new church or replant an old one.

Should a Pastor Be Ordained?

The concept of ordination is, simply, man-made and is neither supported nor forbidden in Scripture. Therefore, while the concept of ordination may not necessarily be bad, it is also not necessary. The closest thing we see in the New Testament to ordination is where the elders of a church lay hands on a new leader and commission him into church leadership.[1] At Mars Hill we do commission our new leaders into ministry by publicly laying hands on them and praying over them. We also license them as legal pastors with our state.

While the Bible does not require ordination, it does require that we obey the laws of our nation and state.[2] In addition to the requirements of the federal government, various state governments have requirements for pastors and churches that are to be obeyed.

1. 1 Tim. 4:14; 5:22.
2. Rom. 13:1–7.

What about Apostles?

There is much confusion regarding the spiritual gift of apostleship because there is sometimes a failure to distinguish between the office of apostle and the gift of apostleship. In the Gospels, the office of apostle refers to the men chosen by Jesus.[3] The requirements for the office of apostle included being an eyewitness to the life and resurrection of Jesus. Thus, apostles of that kind do not exist today and cannot write books of the Bible to record their eyewitness testimony about Jesus.[4] Another requirement is miraculous power.[5]

In addition to the twelve, Romans, 1 Corinthians, 2 Corinthians, Galatians, Ephesians, Colossians, 1 Timothy, 2 Timothy, and Titus all open with Paul introducing himself as an apostle chosen by Jesus. A reading of Acts also shows how Paul ministered cross-culturally and planted churches. Peter held the office of apostle as well.[6]

Although we do not have apostles in the vein of Paul and Peter today, the function of their office does continue in a limited sense. For example, apostleship is referred to as a spiritual gift[7] and refers in a secondary sense to such people as Barnabas,[8] Apollos and Sosthenes,[9] Andronicus and Junias,[10] James,[11] and Silas and Timothy.[12] They, like apostles today, were gifted individuals sent out to move

3. Matt. 10:1; 19:28; 20:17; Mark 3:13–19; 6:7; 9:35; 10:32; Luke 6:12–16; 8:1; 9:1; 22:19–30; John 6:70–71; Rev. 21:14.
4. Acts 1:21–26.
5. Acts 2:43; 5:12; 8:18; 2 Cor. 12:12; Heb. 2:4.
6. Gal. 2:8; 1 Pet. 1:1.
7. 1 Cor. 12:28; Eph. 4:11.
8. Acts 14:3–4, 14.
9. 1 Cor. 1:1; 4:6–9.
10. Rom. 16:7.
11. Gal. 1:19.
12. 1 Thess. 1:1; 2:6.

from place to place in order to plant and establish local churches.[13] This gift also includes the capacity to minister cross-culturally.[14] Today, church planters and missionaries operate out of their gift of apostleship, as well as those Christian leaders God raises up to lead and influence multiple churches and pastors as movement leaders.

Ultimately, the apostle Paul and the twelve apostles in the early church and those gifted with the lesser role of apostle in the present day are not spiritual authorities unto themselves, but rather under the leadership of Jesus, whom Hebrews 3:1 calls "the apostle." Tragically, cult leaders and erroneous teachers who refuse to obey godly church authorities say that they have authority in effect equal to Scripture because they are apostles just like those who wrote the Bible. Such people are condemned in Scripture as "false apostles"[15] and delusional "super-apostles."[16]

How Are the Church Leaders Held Accountable?

In an age of incredible sin among pastors, some of it very public and damaging to the reputation of Christianity, this is a vitally important question.

First, a leader must fear God and be accountable to him. Simply, if any Christian, including a pastor, does not fear God and walk closely with Jesus, then there is truly nothing that can be done to keep him or her from acting in an evil manner. Second, leaders must be accountable to their spouse if they are married. No one knows how we are doing better than our spouse. Third, a leader must be accountable to the other leaders in close relationships marked by honest answers to tough questions. Among the elders this also means that our wives are close and are given

13. Acts 13:3–4.
14. Acts 10:34–35; Eph. 3:7–8.
15. 2 Cor. 11:13; Rev. 2:2.
16. 2 Cor. 11:5; 12:11.

the freedom to speak openly about the condition of their marriages and homes with one another so that there is never any hiding of sin among our elder teams. Fourth, leaders must be in good relations with the leaders of other godly churches in their area to practice unity on the local level as a witness to the city about the unity of God's people. Fifth, leaders must also respect whatever additional accountability structures are needed, including denominational leadership, personal life coaching, or a biblical counselor.

How Should Church Leaders Conduct Church Discipline?

Sadly, there is very little written on the subject of church discipline because so few churches actually practice it with any degree of consistency. Worse still, with few exceptions, most of the books on church discipline that I have read are based upon tragic exegetical errors. It is a common error for Matthew 18:15–22 to be used as some sort of blueprint for how to deal with all church-related sin when that was not its original intent. That text only deals with personal offenses and is only one of a spectrum of Scriptures that speaks to other kinds of sin and how they are to be dealt with. For example, if a woman is raped by a man, the last thing I would encourage her to do is go to the man one on one like Matthew 18:15–22 states for a personal offense. To do so would be to endanger her yet again when the solution is to call the police because a crime has been committed and Romans 13:1–5 is to be followed.

With great wisdom, the Bible provides multiple responses to various people and their sins and heresies. This requires Christians and Christian leaders to use great discernment so they can apply the correct process to each situation rather than either avoiding church discipline altogether or seeking to resolve all issues in the same manner (such as tragically applying Matthew 18:15–22 to more than matters of personal offense).[17]

In summary, the objectives of church discipline from Scripture include the following:

1. When sin has come between people, the goal is repentance and reconciliation.
2. When a wrong has been committed, the goal is resolution and recompense.
3. Church leaders must always pursue the protection of the gospel's reputation and the well-being of the entire church, not just the interests of individual people who have sinned. This explains why sometimes individuals must be put out of the church.[18]
4. Christian leaders are given authority over such matters in the church and must be careful not to in any way abuse the power that God has entrusted to them.[19]
5. Discipline is unpleasant but, in the end, produces a holy people by distinguishing between the world and the church.[20]
6. The goal of church discipline is to make people self-disciplined, which is what it means to be a disciple of Jesus.[21]
7. All matters in the church, including church discipline, are to be done in a fitting and orderly manner.[22]

17. At some point I hope to write an entire book on this subject. For the time being, here are some free resources on church discipline: http://www.marshillchurch.org/audio/mhspecial_church_discipline_16k.mp3 and http://www.marshillchurch.org/audio/A29 Regional_Church Discipline 0406_final.pdf.

18. Deut. 17:7; 19:19; 21:21; 22:24; 24:7; 1 Cor. 5:13, cf. 2 Cor. 2:5–11; Rev. 2:2.

19. 1 Pet. 5:1–5.

20. Heb. 12:11.

21. Gal. 5:23.

22. 1 Cor. 14:40.

8. Because the situations causing church discipline can be incredibly frustrating, it is important that those involved don't let their anger lead them into sin.[23]

9. For the truth to emerge, both sides of a dispute must be heard before a decision is reached.[24]

10. When at all possible, multiple witnesses should be required.[25]

11. The communion table is a regular time appointed by God when his people are to be reminded that unrepentant sin and unnecessary division in the church are unacceptable to a holy God; therefore, urgent matters are to be settled before partaking of the Lord's Supper.[26]

How Does Someone Become a Deacon?

At our church, the deacons are appointed by the elders according to the biblical qualifications and according to the needs of the church. The process of becoming a deacon at our church is similar to that of an elder, but takes less time to complete.

What Are the Terms of Elders and Deacons?

In some churches, elders and deacons are appointed for set terms, often around three years. At Mars Hill we do not have terms, as we see no precedent in Scripture for such time limitations upon our leaders. Additionally, the turnover inherent in the institution of terms causes discontinuity in decision-making and oversight as projects, people, and needs in the church do not magically go away every three years thereby allowing new leaders to take over.

23. Prov. 16:32; 17:27.
24. Prov. 18:17.
25. Deut. 19:15; 2 Cor. 13:1.
26. 1 Cor. 11:17–32.

Our elders are expected to give their lives to service in our church unless God should call them away to serve elsewhere, they should disqualify themselves in some way, or through such reasons as health they are simply unable to perform their duties. We do grant elders seasons of Sabbath as needed to rest during circumstances such as an illness in their family. However, by failure of conduct or performance, men have been removed as elders.

Our deacons serve under a combination of options regarding the duration of their labor. Some deacons are appointed to specific tasks, and so once their task is completed they do not continue functioning as a deacon unless they are re-assigned to another task. Some deacons serve in their area of ministry unless or until life circumstances, such as marriage, the birth of a child, or a move out of Seattle, require them to step down as deacons. Still other deacons oversee areas of ministry that are ongoing and will remain in their position indefinitely.

So, while there is no clear answer to this question in Scripture, God seems to intend that each church answer this question in a way that is most beneficial for the success of their mission.

Are Not Deborah, Priscilla, and Lydia Examples of Female Pastors?

Those people who argue that a woman should hold the highest office of leadership in the church (elder-pastor) often insist that godly women such as Deborah,[27] Priscilla,[28] and Lydia[29] are precedent-setters for us to follow because they were each vitally used by God in ministry. While brevity prevents a lengthy explanation, the issue is really quite simple.

27. Judges 4.
28. Acts 18; Rom. 16:3; 1 Cor. 16:19; 2 Tim. 4:19.
29. Acts 16:11–15.

Deborah was a godly woman raised up by God at one of the lowest spiritual points in the history of Israel because godly men had abdicated their responsibilities. She did hold the leadership positions of judge and prophetess, though she did not occupy the highest position of leadership, the priesthood. Deborah clearly wanted a man to lead, but the men were weak and cowardly, a fact she even disgustedly pointed out to the man Barak. However, Deborah received wisdom from God and gave it to Barak who then led the men into battle, as Deborah—even when leading—selected a man to lead the men. In Deborah we see that, upon occasion, God would rather work with a godly woman than a godless man, though the highest levels of leadership remain reserved solely for men. Similarly, a man is the head of his home, but should he die or leave and thereby abdicate his duties, his wife assumes that responsibility by default.

Priscilla was a godly woman who did ministry side by side with her husband Aquila, including teaching people, like the great preacher Apollos, in their home. While we do not see that she is ever considered a pastor-elder, we do see her leading in the church under the elders, like Paul. By her example we see that godly married couples who do ministry together are invaluable to the church.

Lydia was a godly woman who was apparently unmarried and therefore the head of her household, which included her servants. She was likely a wealthy woman who housed and funded one of Paul's church plants. She is never called an elder-pastor, but from her we see how vital the contributions of a godly woman are to gospel ministry.

In each example we see godly women being used by the Lord for incredible ministry. What we do not see is that they held the highest office of spiritual leadership over God's people, such as the priesthood in the Old Testament or eldership in the New Testament.

Does Not Galatians 3:28 Open the Door for Women to Be Elders?

Perhaps the greatest evangelical feminism battering-ram is found in Galatians 3:28, which says, "There is neither Jew nor Greek, there is neither slave nor free, there is no male nor female, for you are all one in Christ Jesus." The thrust of the feminist argument is that, upon becoming a Christian, such things as gender and culture are obliterated, therefore meaning that such things as gender roles in the family and church are no longer binding upon Christians. But that is not what Paul is saying, as the context of the verse is speaking of inequalities. While much can be said, for the sake of brevity, a few points should make the meaning of this verse clear.

First, we must note that gender distinctions between men and women are a product of creation and not culture, and are therefore binding upon everyone.[30] Second, we must note that Paul is speaking here of the radical equality of men and women "in Christ Jesus," which refers to justification (becoming a Christian), which is the theme of the entire book. Elsewhere, Paul does speak of the functional subordination of wives to their husbands in the home[31] and functional subordination of both men and women to male elders in the church.[32] Third, Paul was possibly responding to a familiar Jewish prayer in which men would thank God that they were not slaves, Greeks, or women, and Paul is arguing that all of God's people are equally loved by him and created by him with their gender, culture, and social status. Fourth, when someone becomes a Christian he or she does not cease to be a man or woman (hence Paul addressing men and women in his letters[33]), cease to be of a particular ethnicity (hence the debate between Gentile and Jew throughout Galatians and the appearance of all

30. Gen. 1:27; Matt. 19:4; Mark 10:6; 1 Tim. 2:11–14.
31. Eph. 5:22–24; Col. 3:18.
32. Acts 20:28; 1 Cor. 11:2–12; 1 Thess. 5:12; 1 Tim. 3:1–7; Titus 1:6–9; Heb. 13:17.
33. For example, Titus 2:1–6.

nations in heaven[34]), or cease to be obligated to their slavery.[35] Slavery in Paul's day may have included up to one-third of the population and was entered through purchase, indebtedness, war capture, and birth.

Jesus has not abolished our distinctions, but rather our inequalities. In short, the issue is not one's gender, one's race or culture, or one's social status, but whether or not one has trusted in Jesus alone for one's salvation. All of God's people are to be united as one family in Christian community and no longer divided into factions of gender, race, culture, social status, employment, or income.

How Large Should an Elder Team Be?

The Bible never speaks to this issue. It is therefore a practical decision that each elder team has to make, factoring in lines of communication, management, and practical issues such as keeping everyone informed and on mission. Ideally, every qualified man who aspires to eldership would be allowed to pursue it so as to allow fresh leaders to help lead the church and encourage new men to rise up as elders. If a church is continually sending out church planters, then there is also a healthy release valve for a burgeoning elder team.

How Should Voting Be Conducted among Elders?

The Bible never speaks to this issue. One line of thinking requires unanimity to ensure a unified team, but this can lead to slow decision-making and one person constantly hitting the brakes on the elder team. Another line of thinking requires consensus, where a team agrees to move together and if someone is not in line they agree to submit to the team or abstain from the voting. Other options include a simple majority of

34. For example, Revelation 5:9; 21:24–26.
35. 1 Cor. 7:20–24; Col. 3:22; Titus 2:9–10; Philem. 8–21.

two-thirds or three-quarters, which has the possibility of leading to division and factions though it speeds up the approval process. Each elder team must wrestle with this issue and come to an agreement on how it votes and why it votes that way. We have found that various issues require different voting thresholds to pass a motion.

What Does Mutual Submission and True Team-Eldering Look Like?

This does not mean that each man does the same things or shares the same level of prominence. What it does mean is that each elder is in fact a respected peer, vital to the team for the contributions he makes. This also means that when one elder sees something concerning (e.g., sin, burnout, discouragement) in another elder, he functions as a pastor and speaks into the life of the other elder, and his input is humbly welcomed. For this to happen, every elder must be in an accountable friendship with another elder, and the elders' wives need the same with other elders' wives so that there is a safe, supportive, and accountable place for elder families to be pastored.

Does an Elder Team Require a Split Pulpit?

Generally, a split pulpit does not function well on the practical level. While Scripture does not forbid this, if a church has multiple gifted preachers, it seems most wise to plant churches and allow each man to maximize his gifts, like the church at Antioch did.[36] At our church I preach most of the time, and when I am out the other elders cover our multiple services at our multiple campuses.

What Wage Should Be Given to a Paid Elder?

The only criteria for the payment of an elder is that an elder be paid in accordance with his worth as a means of showing respect, including a higher wage for the elder

36. Acts 13:1–3.

who carries the pulpit.[37] Many variables will affect the pastor's salary, such as church size, other compensation (e.g., housing allowance, education, books, medical, dental, retirement), tenure, responsibility, performance, family size, and other mitigating circumstances (e.g., a special-needs child). Ideally, any pastor who is full-time should not need to have his wife work outside of the home to generate financial provision for the family.[38] Furthermore, any paid pastor will ideally be compensated sufficiently enough to live near the church he pastors so he can be close to his mission field. An exegetical study of 1 Corinthians 9:1–17 and 1 Timothy 5:17–25 would be most helpful for those seeking a more thorough answer to this question.

How Much Time Should an Unpaid Elder Be Expected to Give to the Church?

This needs to be determined up front so that there is no confusion. Each man's overall life must be considered so that his priorities remain intact. The church must be a priority, but the man also has to care for his family and earn his income, so these responsibilities must be weighed on a case-by-case basis. If a good man simply lacks sufficient time to lead an area of ministry, he should either reorganize his life, take responsibility for a less-demanding area of oversight, or not become an elder.

What Is the Role of the Elders' Wives?

Churches tend to err in one of two ways regarding elders' wives. Some churches elevate the elders' wives to quasi-elders who sit in the business meetings and weigh in on church matters along with their husbands, or worse still, have some goofy co-pastorate, which in prosperity circles is a way to get two incomes and two tax deductions in Jesus' name. In other churches, the elders' wives are not expected to have any mean-

37. 1 Tim. 5:17–18.
38. 1 Tim. 5:8.

ingful connection in the church and in some cases are not even expected to attend the church.

Nonetheless, this is a very important question. The elders' wives should not be treated as some sort of leadership team in and of themselves or be ignored without any expectations. Rather, it should be expected that the elders' wives are mature Christians who are involved in the church according to their gifts and as they and their husbands discern is appropriate for their family. This should not be at the expense of building their walk with God, intimacy with their husband, nurturing of their children, and building of their home to be an example for the other women in the church.[39] As such, they should be faithful church members who are supportive of their husbands and hospitable with their husbands. Sometimes, this means that an elder's wife with a lot of young children and homeward responsibilities may not be an active leader in the church, as her primary ministry is to care for her elder-husband, a ministry that the church should honor and encourage. Other times, an elder's wife may become a deacon, a church employee, or even do ministry such as counseling couples alongside her husband, much like Priscilla and Aquila did throughout the New Testament. At Mars Hill, the elders' wives enjoy prayer, support, friendship, accountability, and encouragement because we believe the health of our elders' marriages and families is a vital safeguard for the health of our church.

What Should I Do if I Disagree with How My Church Is Led and Organized?

You need to begin by searching the Scriptures to make sure that your convictions are true, searching your heart to make sure that your attitude is humble, and searching your motives to make sure that they are to lovingly build up your church.

39. Titus 2:3–5.

If you still disagree with how your church is organized and governed, you should humbly speak with one of the senior leaders in a way that is respectful, not demanding, and not divisive. You should lovingly articulate your concerns and desire to see everything done in a way that honors Jesus according to Scripture, including the organizational structure of the church government.

At this point your church leader may agree and bring your thoughts for the consideration of the other senior leaders. Or, they may disagree with you. In the case that your church is unwilling or unable (because of something such as a legal denominational obligation) to operate in a certain manner to change, then you are left with two options.

First, you can stay in your church and lovingly submit to the leaders and structures that are in place, seeking as best as you are able to build up your church and see it grow in its ability to seek the transformation of your city. Second, you can kindly and lovingly leave your church in a way that is not divisive or disrespectful and attend another church where you can submit to both the church leaders and their form of church government in good conscience.

I offer one final word of caution for the idealistic neatniks who may read this: every church is filled with imperfect people like you who are led by imperfect leaders like me and governed by imperfect systems like the ones outlined in this book. The goal for yourself, your church, and its leaders must be faithfulness and not perfection, so it behooves you to start drinking decaf and to lighten up a bit in Jesus' name.

Appendix 2

Further Reading on Church Leadership

The following books and magazines have been personally enriching to me as a pastor, and I commend them to my fellow church leaders for their benefit, along with any good biography you can find on men such as Jonathan Edwards, Martin Luther, John Calvin, John Chrysostom, Athanasius, and Charles Haddon Spurgeon.

Baxter, Richard. *The Reformed Pastor*. Whitefish, MT: Kessinger, 2007.

Beck, James R., and Craig L. Blomberg, eds. *Two Views on Women in Ministry*. Grand Rapids, MI: Zondervan, 2005.

Bickel, R. Bruce. *Light and Heat: The Puritan View of the Pulpit*. Orlando, FL: Soli Deo Gloria, 1999.

Chapell, Bryan. *Christ-Centered Preaching: Redeeming the Expository Sermon*. Grand Rapids, MI: Baker, 2005.

Clowney, Edmund P. *Preaching Christ in All of Scripture*. Wheaton, IL: Crossway, 2003.

Dever, Mark, and Paul Alexander. *The Deliberate Church: Building Your Ministry on the Gospel*. Wheaton, IL: Crossway, 2005.

Dever, Mark. *Nine Marks of a Healthy Church*. Wheaton, IL: Crossway, 2004.

Dickson, David. *The Elder and His Work*. Edited by George Kennedy McFarland and Philip Graham Ryken. Phillipsburg, NJ: P&R, 2004.

Getz, Gene A. *Elders and Leaders*. Chicago, IL: Moody, 2003.

Goldsworthy, Graeme. *Preaching the Whole Bible as Christian Scripture: The Application of Biblical Theology to Expository Preaching*. Grand Rapids, MI: Eerdmans, 2000.

Greidanus, Sidney. *Preaching Christ from the Old Testament: A Contemporary Hermeneutical Method*. Grand Rapids, MI: Eerdmans, 1999.

Harvard Business Review (www.harvardbusinessreview.com).

Leadership Journal (www.leadershipjournal.net).

Lloyd-Jones, D. Martyn. *Preaching and Preachers*. Grand Rapids, MI: Zondervan, 1972.

Myra, Harold, and Marshall Shelley. *The Leadership Secrets of Billy Graham*. Grand Rapids, MI: Zondervan, 2005.

Osborne, Larry W. *The Unity Factor*. Vista, CA: Owl's Nest, 2001.

Peterson, Eugene H. *The Contemplative Pastor: Returning to the Art of Spiritual Direction*. Grand Rapids, MI: Eerdmans, 1989.

Peterson, Eugene H. *Working the Angles: The Shape of Pastoral Integrity*. Grand Rapids, MI: Eerdmans, 1987.

Piper, John. *Brothers, We Are Not Professionals: A Plea to Pastors for Radical Ministry*. Nashville: Broadman & Holman, 2002.

Spurgeon, Charles H. *Lectures to My Students*. Grand Rapids, MI: Zondervan, 1972.

Stetzer, Ed, and David Putnam. *Breaking the Missional Code: Your Church Can Become a Missionary in Your Community*. Nashville: Broadman & Holman, 2006.

Stott, John. *The Living Church: Convictions of a Lifelong Pastor*. Downers Grove, IL: InterVarsity Press, 2007.

Strauch, Alexander. *Biblical Eldership: An Urgent Call to Restore Biblical Church Leadership*. Colorado Springs, CO: Lewis & Roth, 2005.

Wilson, Douglas. *Mother Kirk: Essays and Forays in Practical Ecclesiology*. Moscow, ID: Canon Press, 2001.

At the risk of self-promoting, I have written two books that may also be of help for church leaders.

Driscoll, Mark. *Confessions of a Reformission Rev.: Hard Lessons from an Emerging Missional Church*. Grand Rapids, MI: Zondervan, 2006.

Driscoll, Mark. *The Radical Reformission: Reaching Out without Selling Out*. Grand Rapids, MI: Zondervan, 2004.

Appendix 3

Sample Church Membership Covenant

Mars Hill Church Membership Covenant

Introduction

> Present your bodies as a living sacrifice, holy and acceptable to God, which is your spiritual worship. Do not be conformed to this world, but be transformed by the renewal of your mind, that by testing you may discern what is the will of God, what is good and acceptable and perfect (Rom. 12:1–2).

As Christians, we are members of God's household (Eph. 2:19) called to function, participate, and minister in a particular place within the body of Christ. A healthy body requires that each member does its part well. A healthy church requires the same: members who are sacrificially committed and well equipped to do the works of service that God has prepared in advance for them to do (Eph. 2:10; 4:12). Mars Hill Church holds its members in high regard; we expect them to lead as missionaries of the gospel to the culture. God, in his sovereignty, placed us in this city, among these people, in this century, for a reason (Acts 17:26–27).

> For by the grace given to me I say to everyone among you not to think of himself more highly than he ought to think, but to think with sober judgment, each according to the measure of faith that God has assigned. For as in one body we have many members, and the members do not all have the same function, so we, though many, are one body

in Christ, and individually members one of another. Having gifts that differ according to the grace given to us, let us use them (Rom. 12:3–8).

Being a member of Mars Hill Church is really about being part of a family. All members are disciples of Jesus, unified by their identity in Christ. This unity is expressed in the way they collaborate in loving God, loving fellow Christians, and loving non-Christians. Members who enter into a covenant with their local church are called to a higher degree of responsibility and service. At the same time, the elders and deacons are covenanted to assist members first and foremost, to love and lead, provide counsel and aid, and pray for, teach, and guide them.

> Above all, keep loving one another earnestly, since love covers a multitude of sins. Show hospitality to one another without grumbling. As each has received a gift, use it to serve one another, as good stewards of God's varied grace (1 Pet. 4:8–10).

What Is a Covenant?

A covenant is a promise by which we obligate ourselves to one another in such a way that the obligation of one party is not dependent on the faithfulness of the other (Ps. 76:11; Ezek. 20:44; 36:22; Hos. 2:19–20; 3:1; 2 Tim. 2:13). The Mars Hill Church covenant includes a statement of faith, a statement of biblical doctrine, the obligations of Mars Hill Church to its members, and the obligations of members to Mars Hill Church. Though the covenant does define the relationship between members and the church, it is first and foremost a promise made to God as a commitment to his glory and his bride, the church (Eph. 5:25).

Statement of Faith

- I am a Christian saved from the eternal wrath of God by faith in Jesus Christ, my Lord and Savior, through his death and resurrection, by which I am assured of eternal life (John 3:16–18; Rom. 3:23–26).
- I believe Jesus Christ is exactly who he claimed to be (Isa. 5:6; Matt. 26:64; Mark 14:62; Luke 22:70; John 4:25–26; 6:29; 8:58; 11:25–27; 14:6–7; 15:5).
- I have repented of my sins and have been made a new creation in Christ (2 Cor. 5:17; 1 John 1:9).
- In obedience to Scripture, I have been baptized to personally identify with the death, burial, and resurrection of Jesus, and to publicly demonstrate my commitment as a disciple of Jesus (Col. 2:12; 1 Pet. 3:21).

Statement of Biblical Doctrine

- I agree with the core beliefs of Mars Hill Church, which are founded upon historic creeds (e.g., Apostles' Creed and Nicene Creed) and expressed in the Mars Hill doctrinal statement.
- I understand the importance of submission to church leadership and will be diligent to preserve unity and peace; I will adhere to Mars Hill Church's position on primary theological issues, and I will not be divisive over secondary issues (Eph. 4:1–3; Heb. 13:7, 17).
- I agree that the sixty-six books of the Bible are the ultimate doctrinal authority on all matters (Isa. 55:11; 1 Cor. 15:3–4; 2 Tim. 3:15–16; Heb. 4:12).
- I understand that Mars Hill Church doctrine is also communicated and specified through various channels, such as sermons, published materials, and other writings distributed by Mars Hill Church.

Obligation of Mars Hill Church to Its Members

- We covenant that your elders and deacons will meet the criteria assigned to them in the Scriptures (1 Tim. 3:1–13; 5:17–22; Titus 1:5–9; 1 Pet. 5:1–4).
- We covenant to seek God's will for our church community to the best of our ability as we study the Scriptures and follow the Spirit (Acts 20:28; 1 Pet. 5:1–5).
- We covenant to care for you and seek your growth as a disciple of Christ, in part by equipping you for service (Eph. 4:11–13) and praying for you regularly, particularly when you are sick (James 5:14).
- We covenant to provide teaching and counsel from the whole of Scripture (Acts 20:27–28; Gal. 6:6, 1 Tim. 5:17–18).
- We covenant to be on guard against false teachers (Acts 20:28–31).
- We covenant to exercise church discipline when necessary (Matt. 18:15–20; 1 Corinthians 5; Gal. 6:1).
- We covenant to set an example and join you in fulfilling the duties of church members (1 Cor. 11:1; Phil. 3:17; 1 Tim. 4:12).

My Obligation to Mars Hill Church as a Member

- I have read and understood the Mars Hill doctrinal statement and will not be divisive to its teaching. I also understand the importance of submission to church leadership and will be diligent to preserve unity and peace (Eph. 4:1–3; Heb. 13:7, 17).
- I covenant to submit to the authority of Scripture as the final arbiter on all issues (Psalm 119; 2 Tim. 3:16–17).

- I will maintain a close relationship with the Lord Jesus through regular Bible reading, prayer, fellowship, and practice of spiritual disciplines. My relationship will be evident through my participation in weekly worship services, communion, Mars Hill community, service, and a life that glorifies Jesus (Pss. 105:1–2; 119:97; Acts 2:42–47; Heb. 10:23–25; 2 Pet. 1:3).

- I will steward the resources God has given me, including my time, talents, and treasure (Prov. 3:9–10; Rom. 12:1–2; Gal. 5:22–26; Eph. 4:1–16; 5:15–18). This includes regular financial giving, service, and participation in community that is sacrificial, cheerful, and voluntary (Rom. 12:1–8; 2 Cor. 8–9; 12:7–31; 1 Pet. 4:10–11).

- I will not function in leadership or as a member in another church family (Heb. 13:17).

- I covenant to submit to discipline by God through his Holy Spirit, to follow biblical procedures for church discipline in my relationships with brothers and sisters in Christ, to submit to righteous discipline when approached biblically by brothers and sisters in Christ, and to submit to discipline by church leadership if the need should ever arise (Ps. 141:5; Matt. 18:15–17; 1 Cor. 5:1–5; 2 Cor. 2:5–8; Gal. 6:1–5, 8; 1 Tim. 5:20; 2 Tim. 2:25; Titus 1:9; 3:10–11; Heb. 12:5–11; Rev. 2:5–7, 14–25).

- I agree, by God's grace, to walk in holiness as an act of worship to Jesus Christ, who has saved me from my sin so that I could live a new life (2 Cor. 5:17). I will practice complete chastity before marriage and complete fidelity in heterosexual marriage by abstaining from practices such as cohabitation, pornography, and fornication (Job 31:1; Proverbs 5; Rom. 13:12–14; 1 Cor. 6:9–7:16; Heb. 13:4). I will refrain from illegal drug use, drunkenness, and other sinful behavior as the Bible, my pastors, and my conscience dictate (1 Cor. 8:7; Gal. 5:19–21). Should I sin in such a manner, I agree to confess my sins to Christian brothers or sisters and seek help to put my sin to death (Rom. 8:13; Col. 3:5; 1 John 1:6–10).

My Commitment to the Mission of Mars Hill Church

Mars Hill Mission Statement: *Mars Hill Church lives for Jesus as a city within the city: knowing culture, loving people, and seeing lives transformed to live for Jesus.*

I have read the mission statement of Mars Hill Church and commit to live out this mission as a diligent, faithful disciple of Jesus, that my identity would be in him, my worship would be for him, my fellowship would be through him, and my interaction with the culture would be for his glory.

I understand that this covenant obligates me to the members of Mars Hill and is an acknowledgement of my submission to the elders of the church. I accept the responsibility to notify Mars Hill leadership if at any time I can no longer commit to this covenant, or if I have any questions, comments, or concerns regarding Mars Hill Church.

Pastor Mark Driscoll founded Mars Hill Church (www.marshillchurch.org) in Seattle in the fall of 1996, which has grown to over six thousand people in one of America's least churched cities. He co-founded and is president of the Acts 29 Church Planting Network (www.acts29network.org), which has planted over one hundred churches in the United States and internationally. Most recently he founded the Resurgence Missional Theology Cooperative (www.theresurgence.com).

Outreach magazine has recognized Mars Hill Church as the second most innovative, twenty-third fastest-growing, and second most prolific church-planting church in America. *The Church Report* has recognized Pastor Mark as the eighth most influential pastor in America. His sermons are downloaded a few million times a year. *Seattle* magazine has named Pastor Mark one of the twenty-five most powerful people in Seattle.

Media coverage on Pastor Mark and Mars Hill varies from National Public Radio to *Mother Jones* magazine, the *Associated Press*, the *New York Times*, *Blender* music magazine, *Outreach* magazine, *Christianity Today*, *Preaching Today*, and *Leadership* magazine to ABC Television and the 700 Club.

His writing includes the books *Vintage Jesus, The Radical Reformission: Reaching Out without Selling Out* and *Confessions of a Reformission Rev.: Hard Lessons from an Emerging Missional Church*. He also contributed to the books *The Supremacy of Christ in a Postmodern World* and *Listening to the Beliefs of Emerging Churches*. Most enjoyably, Mark and his high school sweetheart, Grace, delight in raising their three sons and two daughters.